UKRAINIAN HOME COOKING

FAVORITE RECIPES SEASONED WITH LOVE

Photographer Alona Bogdanova
Translator Aleksandra Kolesnikova
Editor Shawnn Welde
Book designer Anna Syvolozhska
Cover designer Svitlana Stefaniuk

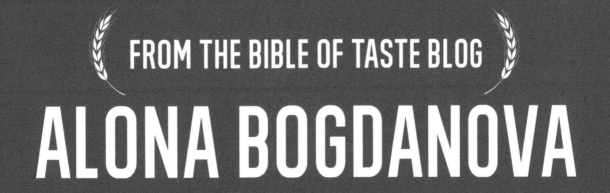

FROM THE BIBLE OF TASTE BLOG

ALONA BOGDANOVA

Introduction

Ukrainian cuisine is part of the national cultural heritage, along with the language, literature, and art. Ukrainians appreciate and take great pride in their national cooking, which is a real treasure inherited from past generations. Today, Ukraine is eager to share it with the rest of the world with both gratitude and love.

Ukrainian cuisine has gone a long way in absorbing cooking traditions of different nations. It was influenced by the country's geography, nature, and climate conditions. Ethnically, Ukraine is a very diverse country, which is another factor that greatly influenced the national traditional cooking. Constant interchange and family ties between different ethnic groups eventually encouraged many local traditions to meld and become common for the whole country.

With its centuries-old history, Ukrainian cooking is very diverse, delicious, and highly nutritious. Most recipes involve many components that undergo complex processing.

Mountainous areas of Zakarpattia are favorable for raising livestock and making dairy products. Low-lying plains with a mild climate are good for growing grain and staple vegetables. Besides, the forests and hills of Zakarpattia are rich in mushrooms, berries, fruit, and game. There are plenty of fish in the rivers, too. A number of fish farms in the region raise trout, carp, etc.

Agriculture has always thrived in Ukraine, with its favorable geography and climate conditions. Wheat from the north and rye from the south grow equally well here, as well as oats, buckwheat, barley, peas, beans, various vegetables, fruits, and berries. Corn, potatoes, and tomatoes were easily adopted in Ukraine, too.

The way food is thermally processed is one of the key elements in any national cuisine, and it largely depends on the design of the fireplace used in people's dwellings. Ukrainians used a closed masonry hearth (a stove). So they mostly had their food boiled, stewed or baked. A lot of ingredients experience complex heat processing — first they are fried or boiled, then they are stewed or baked. This is a distinctive feature of Ukrainian cooking. Complex heat processing helps to preserve the flavor of the dishes and makes them juicy.

Stoves were multifunctional. Apart from cooking, they were also used for heating. A stove was mostly used for boiling and stewing, as well as for baking bread. During their long journeys, chumaks (merchants who carried salt on ox-drawn carts from the faraway Azov coast and Crimea) used to build kabytsia — a temporary stove in the ground with a chimney and draft mechanism. They used those stoves to cook kulish (millet porridge with salo, onion and garlic), porridge, lemishka (simmered buckwheat flour), halushky (thick, soft dumplings) and game soups. During their military campaigns, Zaporozhian Cossacks cooked food in the same way as well. Even hunters used to make yushka (a clear soup) with the game they caught rather than roast the meat on an open fire.

Both plants and meat have always been a part of the Ukrainian diet. Wheat, barley and millet were the first grain crops grown in Ukraine. Rye appeared much later.

Besides various flour-based dishes and cereals, Ukrainians ate a lot of pulses and combined them with vegetables and fruit. Meat, however, was long considered to be festive food. Historically, Ukrainians have always preferred pork among all kinds of meat, and salo (cured fatback) has always been the most widespread animal fat. Moreover, Ukrainian peasants enriched their diet with fish, mushrooms, wild berries and fruit. Fish, such as carp, bream, catfish, tench, and pike, played a significant part in Ukrainian ancestors' nourishment. Caviar of different species of fish was used as well.

Ukrainians used to eat a lot of millet as part of various dishes. Wheat and other kinds of cereal were widely used to make kutia (traditional Christmas dish). Rice was also imported to Ukraine. Unleavened dough was used to make halushky and bake different kinds of bread, pies and kalach (ring-shaped braided bread). Animal fat was popular in Ukrainian cooking.

Great attention has always been paid to the foodflavor. When cooking, Ukrainian housewives used spices such as black and red pepper, allspice, caraway, garlic and horseradish. Almost every dish was sprinkled with parsley, dill, celery, or green onions. In their vegetable gardens people cultivated cabbages, beets, radishes, carrots, cucumbers, and pumpkins. As for fruit and berries, Ukrainians ate apples, cherries, plums, currants, lingonberries, raspberries and cranberries.

Ukrainian cuisine is famous for a variety of sauces and gravies. The most popular desserts are dishes based on cream, eggs, cottage cheese, honey, and fruit. Making homemade preserves is another passed down tradition of Ukrainian households. In order to have vegetables and fruit all year round, Ukrainian women have always made preserves using different methods such as canning, salting, drying and fermentation.

Buckwheat was brought from Asia in XI–XII centuries. It was eaten both as grits and flour. Buckwheat was used

Many distinctive features of Ukrainian cooking stem from the people's way of life. The overwhelming majority of Ukrainians were engaged in heavy agricultural labor. To work hard in the field, people needed nourishing, high-calorie food. That is why Ukrainian dishes are so rich in protein, fats, and carbohydrates. Of course, the food had to be tasty as well, which explains why most Ukrainian dishes involve so many ingredients (for example, in borscht there can be up to twenty components) and combine several methods of heat processing.

to make hrechanyky (buckwheat patties), pastry, halushky, lemishka, porridge, and babka (a kind of casserole). Corn, pumpkins, and beans came to Ukraine from America. Corn was eaten both as grits and flour to bake bread and to cook mamalyha, babka, kulish, kukurudzianka, banosh and many other different dishes.

Pumpkins were eaten baked or boiled with porridge. Asparagus, peppers, celery, and beans were also introduced in Ukrainian cooking eventually.

In the 18th century, potatoes became widely spread in Ukraine and were used to cook soups and main dishes. This vegetable became the "second bread" in the country.

Almost every soup in Ukraine started having potatoes as its permanent component. As a garnish for main courses, potatoes were combined with meat, fish, and vegetables. Besides, people began to make starch from potatoes, which gave Ukrainians a new beverage — kyssil (sweet juice thickened with starch).

Sunflowers and mustard appeared in the 18th century. Since that time, sunflower oil has been the number one cooking oil in Ukraine.

Tomatoes, eggplants and beets were adopted in the 19th century. Eggplants are fried or stewed with other vegetables. They are also used to make eggplant paste, which is another popular dish.

Cane sugar was delivered from abroad, so it was very expensive. That is why Ukrainians used to sweeten their desserts and beverages with honey. However, it wasn't long before beet sugar had appeared and gained popularity in the country. Sugar, fruit, and berries were used to make various alcoholic beverages, such as nalivka and varenukha.

Unfortunately, due to a number of social and economic conditions, Ukrainian cuisine suffered decline. Increased feudal oppression experienced by Ukrainian peasants, frequent crop failures, unbearable tax burden, heavy land acquisition payments that peasants had to make after the "reform" of 1861 — all these factors placed a considerable strain on the Ukrainian people. The subsequent development of capitalism undermined people's nutrition even further. Under such circumstances, Ukrainian national cuisine could not fully preserve its integrity and diversity. Nor could it develop during the Soviet Union period.

Like any other national cuisine with a rich historical past, Ukrainian cooking varies a lot in different regions.

Western Ukrainian cuisine differs greatly from that in Eastern Ukraine. Cooking traditions in Bukovyna were clearly influenced by Turkish cuisine, and Hutsul cuisine bears a strong resemblance to Hungarian cooking. Central Ukrainian cuisine is the most diverse, in particular the central areas of the Right-Bank Ukraine. Borscht, which is the most popular dish in Ukraine, has up to thirty varieties (Poltava, Chernihiv, Kyiv, Volyn, Lviv, etc.). Almost every region in the country has its own recipe. Up to twenty different ingredients are used to cook borscht, which explains its delicious flavor and high nutritional value. A combination of different components comes together in a savory harmonious blend.

Ukrainian cookware and crockery reflect the distinctive features of Ukrainian cooking. There are cauldrons for boiling, deep frying pans, and a large variety of crockery pots for stewing.

Speaking about cooking technologies, all components (and especially meat) are usually chopped, sliced, or shredded in some way. This explains why Ukrainian cuisine has a lot of different meat rolls (kruchenyky or zavyvantsi), stuffed diffes, casseroles, cutlets and meatballs (sichenyky), and other minced meat dishes borrowed from German cooking traditions via Polish and Czech cuisines.

Ukrainian food is usually seasoned with local spices such as onion, garlic, dill, caraway, anise, mint, lovage, angelica, thyme and red pepper. Imported spices such as bay leaf, black pepper, and cinnamon (for sweet dishes) are also widely used. Vinegar plays an important role as a seasoning for meat, cold appetizers, and vegetable dishes. Unfortunately, it is used a bit too often, though.

Cooking traditions in Hutsulshchyna (mountainous areas in Western Ukraine) are both simple and original. The most popular food here is corn grits and cornmeal, potatoes, beans, mushrooms, and, of course, brynza (also called bryndza or bryndzia), which is soft fresh cheese with a strong smell and taste. The iconic Hutsul dish, banush (or banosh), is usually cooked in a cast iron cauldron on an open fire.

Mushroom yushka is a popular soup in this region. The recipe involves boiling dried mushrooms in chicken stock with spices, homemade noodles, and greens.

Hutsul borscht is made with fermented beet and smoked pork.

Hutsul cuisine also has specialities such as huslyanka (fermented milk), vurda (a kind of sheep milk cheese) and shupenia (bean dish).

Zakarpattia cuisine is remarkable for its rich diversity as it unites Ukrainian, Hungarian, Romanian, Slovak, Czech, and other cooking traditions. It has a lot of dishes made from dough, cornmeal, meat, fish, and vegetables. Hungarian cooking is usually rather spicy. Dishes such as hulyash, bograch, and others are generously seasoned with paprika. Zakarpattia's famous dishes are hombovtsi (steamed dessert), bean soups, kremzlyky (potato fritters), and Verkhovyna beans. Kholodets (meat jelly or aspic) is also widespread in Zakarpattia. Here they call it klyahanets. Other popular dishes are mamalyha, paprikash, tokan and lotsi. The latter is made from tenderized pork stewed with onions.

Paprikash is a meat or fish dish with a sour cream sauce seasoned with paprika.

Tokan is beef cooked with bell peppers, mushrooms, vegetables, and spices.

In Halychyna people like vegetable dishes and cold soups (kholodnyky) made from apples, pears, cherries, raspberries, plums, blackberries, etc.

Steamed dishes are cooked with cabbages, potatoes, peas, carrots, pumpkins, spinach, and cauliflower. Boiled and fried green beans are popular in summer.

Other traditional dishes in Halychyna are black pudding (blood sausage or kyshka) with buckwheat, potatoes or liver; salceson (sausage with pork byproducts); pâté made from pork, hare, pigeon, duck, or veal; studenets (meat jelly with brains, liver, pig's trotters, rooster, turkey, etc.).

Ukrainian people like various gravies (pidbyvky or machanky) with mushrooms, chicken, goose, cauliflower, onions, dill, horseradish, parsley, etc.

There is also a great variety of dishes based on grated and boiled potatoes — bulbyanyky, deruny (playtsky), palchyky, knedli, varenyky (pyrohy) with cheese, cabbage, and other ingredients.

Pork cured fatback (salo) is the most popular and widespread food in the Poltava region. People eat it separately or use it for fat and flavor in various dishes. Salo can be eaten raw, salted, boiled, smoked or fried. It can be used as cooking fat, for larding lean meat and even in sweet dishes where it is combined with sugar or molasses.

Poltava cuisine is rich in dishes based on flour and cereal — bublyki (ring-shaped bread rolls), varenyky (stuffed dumplings), halushky, hrechanyky, knyshi and pyrohy (buns stuffed with filling), korzhi (baked unleavened flatbread), pampushky (soft buns with garlic), pundyki (unleavened buns fried in oil), shulyki (honey cookies with poppy seeds). Rice has been popular in Poltava for a very long time. Local people used to call it "Sorochynske millet" (derived from "Saracen", i.e. Turkish).

Holubtsi (cabbage leaves with filling), varenyky, and deruny (potato fritters) have become very popular in Western Ukraine lately, whereas fish, kholodets, and salo are favorites in the central part of the country. Kholodets is widespread in Western Ukraine as well. In northern regions, people are likely to eat more potatoes, various soups, and tovchenyky (dumplings fried with chopped meat), while in the south people prefer pelmeni (meat dumplings), fried potatoes, and plov (pilaf). In Eastern Ukraine and in Donbas they like salads and meat dishes.

Odessa cuisine was influenced by various cooking traditions — Ukrainian, Jewish, Georgian, Armenian, Uzbek, Bulgarian, Moldavian, and Greek.

Since the city is located at the coast, its cuisine has a lot of seafood and fish.

Gefilte fish (usually pike) is the most popular festive dish here. Fried fish is another favorite food. Usually they prefer Black sea plaice and goby fish. Small fishes from the herring fish family (sprats, anchovies) are used to cook fried minced balls.

Forshmak is a widespread appetizer made from salted minced fish. In Odessa they also like stuffed dishes, such as stuffed bell peppers, zucchini, and chicken. Varenyky and holubtsi are usually made smaller in size in this part of the country.

It is not uncommon that the same dishes are cooked differently in various parts of Ukraine. For instance, they don't use beet in borscht in Prymorsk, and in Donetsk this dish looks absolutely different — with cucumbers, boiled eggs, and vinegar. Likewise, there are numerous recipes of okroshka (cold soup with raw vegetables and meat).

Western Ukraine has a classic festive menu that is unimaginable without homemade sausages, and kholodets served with horseradish. In the north of the country they cook pechivo, which is a mix of potatoes, cabbage, and meat stewed in pots in the oven. Deruny is an iconic dish in this region. There is even a monument to this dish in Korosten (Zhytomyr region). The central areas of Ukraine are proud of their halushky. Every household has its family recipe of this popular dish.

Deruny are very popular in Lviv as well. There are numerous recipes for this dish. What is more, this dish has different names in different regions. Here are some of them: tertiukhy, kremzlyky, kyizlyky, tarchanky, and betsi.

In Lviv, varenyky are served with large pieces of fried pork belly, followed by coffee and Lviv syrnyk, which is a local version of cheesecake.

Cooking traditions in the central parts of the country have numerous dishes made of dough. Some of them were even portrayed in literature. For example, varenyky and halushky in Poltava, or pampusky topped with garlic served together with borscht in the Cherkassy region.

Pundyky are very popular in Poltava. These are thin flatbread pieces made from unleavened dough mixed with eggs and kefir, and after that fried together with onions. Pundyky can vary a lot — savory or sweet, or served with sour cream — the truth is that they are all delicious. In Poltava, they also like varenyky and halushky. Nowadays, halushky are often made with filling; for example, with chicken or liver. Varenyky in Poltava are huge — large enough to fit in the palm — and cooked with steam.

In Eastern Ukraine, people like cooking borscht and okroshka. There are lots of recipes of okroshka — based on kvas (fermented cereal-based beverage), whey, kefir or broth, served with mustard and radish or without it. Okroshka is an ideal soup for hot summer weather. As for Dnipro, Jewish dishes are popular here; for instance, forshmak, which is cooked in different ways throughout Ukraine. It can be served with butter, bread, potatoes, or even apples. Mamalyha is a favorite dish in Western Ukraine, whereas northern areas of the country prefer meat stewed with vegetables.

This cookbook shows Ukrainian cuisine in all its rich diversity without regional markers. Welcome, and enjoy the gastronomic tour over united Ukraine!

Contents

Salads and appetizers

Soups, borscht, yushka

Main Dishes

Salads and appetizers

Poltava potato salad

Ingredients

2 potatoes

100 g (3½ oz) pickled stump mushrooms

1 red onion

80 g (3 oz) canned peas

2 tbsp unrefined oil

1 tsp ground black pepper

1/4 tsp mustard

1 tbsp apple cider vinegar

1 tsp powdered sugar

Salt

1. Peel and cut the potatoes the way you want them in the salad. Cover with boiling water and cook until tender. Don't overcook! The potatoes should remain slightly hard.

2. Make the dressing. Mix the mustard, powdered sugar, salt, pepper, oil and vinegar.

3. When the potatoes are cooked through, drain them, rinse with cold water twice. Add the marinade, cover with a lid, and shake the pot to make the potatoes mix with the dressing. Leave to cool.

4. Slice the onion into thin rings, add the peas, mushrooms, and potatoes. Mix everything.

5. Sprinkle with chopped parsley and serve.

Roasted veggies appetizer in a jar

Ingredients

8 portobello mushrooms

1 eggplant

1 bell pepper

2 tomatoes

2 cloves garlic

2 tbsp unrefined oil

Chopped dill

1. Preheat the oven to 220 °C (425 °F).

2. Quarter the bell pepper, remove the seeds and the stem. Clean the mushrooms. Pierce the eggplant every 3 cm (1 in) with a fork. Do not peel the eggplant.

3. Put all the vegetables on a wire rack, except tomatoes and garlic. Roast for 30–40 minutes.

4. Mushrooms take less time to cook, so take them out sooner. Put them into a jar and cover with a lid.

5. Cut a small X on the tomatoes with a knife, dunk them in boiling water from a kettle, and leave for one minute. The skin will slip off. Remove the seeds and dice into cubes.

6. Roast the pepper until its skin gets dark and blistered. The eggplant should become soft.

7. Take all the vegetables out of the oven and put them into the jar immediately. If the eggplant doesn't fit into the jar, cut it into halves. Leave for 20 minutes.

8. Remove the skin from the pepper and the eggplant. It should peel off easily. The steam from the vegetables will make the mushrooms juicier.

9. Dice all the vegetables into equal cubes and mix them with the tomatoes. Squeeze the garlic, add salt and pepper, sprinkle with chopped dill and drizzle with unrefined oil.

Brynza and roasted pepper appetizer

This appetizer is as simple as it is delicious. You can make it even with the most common green peppers. You can simply fry them, flipping from one side to another, without peeling. Let the peppers give off the steam, so that the skin slips off easily, and remove the seeds after that. You can also add a little garlic to the marinade. The peppers can be served without brynza, but this will make an entirely new appetizer. The taste of brynza reveals itself after it is cut into small pieces. It acquires a buttery flavor then. By the way, if the brynza you have appears a bit too hard and not very tasty, mincing it in a blender can save the day.

Ingredients

4 bell peppers

300 g (10½ oz) soft brynza (or any other soft fresh cheese, e.g. ricotta)

1½ tsp salt

1 tbsp powdered sugar

2 tbsp apple cider vinegar

1 tsp ground black pepper

1. Preheat the oven to 220 °C (425 °F).

2. Cut the bell peppers into quarters, remove the seeds and the stem.

3. Put the peppers on a wire rack and place it in the top section of the oven. Roast for 30–40 minutes until the skin gets nicely charred and blistered.

4. Take the peppers out of the oven and immediately put them in a plastic bag, a glass jar, or any other container with a lid. Set aside for 20 minutes.

5. Take out the peppers and remove the skin.

6. Make marinade by mixing together powdered sugar, salt, pepper, and apple cider vinegar. Pour this marinade over the peppers and leave for at least one hour.

7. Mince the brynza in a meat grinder or a blender, or simply crush it with your hands.

8. Arrange the peppers on one side of the plate and put the minced brynza beside them. Season with dill to taste.

Ramson salad

Ingredients

1 bunch ramson

100 g (3½ oz) brynza (or any other soft fresh cheese, e.g. ricotta)

100 g (3½ oz) radish

2 tbsp crushed walnut

1 tsp liquid honey

1. Sort out the ramsons, wash thoroughly, cut off the hard parts and chop.

2. Mash the brynza with your hands. If it is hard, put it through a meat grinder or use a blender.

3. Cut the radishes into thin matchsticks.

4. Combine all the components, add the honey, sprinkle with crushed walnuts and chopped dill.

Sauerkraut and mushroom salad

Ingredients

- 300 g (10½ oz) sauerkraut
- 100 g (3½ oz) pickled stump mushrooms
- 2 tbsp unrefined oil
- Dill
- Green onions

1. Cut the sauerkraut into pieces 3–4 cm (1–2 in) long so that it will be easier to eat.

2. Rinse the mushrooms and mix with the sauerkraut. Add finely chopped dill and green onions.

3. Drizzle with oil and mix.

Beet and spinach salad

Ingredients

- 2 young beets
- 1 big bunch spinach
- 250 g (9 oz) soft brynza (or any other soft fresh cheese, e.g. ricotta)
- 100 g (3½ oz) walnuts
- 2 tbsp oil
- 1 tsp wine vinegar
- 1 tsp powdered sugar
- 1/4 tsp salt

1. Wash the beets, but don't peel. Wrap in foil and bake in the oven at 190 °C (375 °F) for 1½ –2 hours.

2. Unfold the foil and leave the beets to cool. Peel and cut the beets. Add salt, pepper, powdered sugar, oil, and vinegar.

3. Wash the spinach thoroughly to get rid of sand and dry. Mash the brynza with a fork.

4. Crush the walnuts with a knife or in a mortar. Heat on a dry frying pan for 3–4 minutes.

5. Mix the spinach with the beets. Put the brynza and the walnuts on top.

Sauerkraut — Ukrainian fermented cabbage

Ingredients

4 kg (8.8 lb) cabbages

70 g (2½ oz) salt

100 g (3½ oz) carrots

10 bay leaves

1 tbsp peppercorns

1 bunch dill

1. Remove the wilted outer leaves, cut the cabbages in half and shred. You can use a mandoline slicer. Peel and grate the carrots.

2. Wash the container for sauerkraut thoroughly, dry and scald it with boiling water. Traditionally, sauerkraut is fermented in barrels. You can buy a small barrel or use a common glass jar.

3. Thoroughly wash and dry the dill.

4. Combine the shredded cabbage with salt, carrots, pepper, and bay leaves.

5. Put the cabbage into the jar in small batches. Tamp down each batch well. The cabbage juice must appear in the end.

6. Cover with cabbage leaves and tie a piece of cheesecloth loosely so that it sags a little. Put a weight wrapped in a piece of clean cloth on top.

7. A big barrel takes 14 days to ferment. If you make sauerkraut in small jars, it will be ready in 4 days.

Beet and prune salad

Ingredients

500 g (1 lb) beets

100 g (3½ oz) prunes

40 g (1½ oz) walnuts

2 tbsp refined oil

1 tsp apple cider vinegar

2 cloves garlic

Salt

1 tsp powdered sugar

1. Boil the beets with the skin on until they are cooked through. Leave to cool and peel.

2. Pour boiling water over the prunes and leave for 20 minutes.

3. Crush the walnuts with a knife and dry on a frying pan.

4. Cut the beets into matchsticks or grate finely. Drizzle with vinegar and oil. Add salt, powdered sugar, and chopped garlic. Mix everything.

5. Drain the prunes and cut them into matchsticks. Stir the prunes into the beets and serve.

Rustic radish and cucumber salad

Ingredients

3 medium-sized potatoes

150 g (5⅓ oz) radishes

80 g (3 oz) fresh cucumbers

1 tsp apple cider vinegar

1 tbsp honey

2½ tbsp refined oil

1/3 tsp ground black pepper

1/3 tsp mustard

Green onions

Salt

1. Boil the potatoes in jackets. Put them into cold water. This will help to remove the skin. Peel and cut into pieces ½ cm (⅕ in) thick.

2. Combine the mustard with honey, salt, and black pepper. Add oil and vinegar. Pour this dressing over the potatoes. Mix carefully and leave for 20 minutes to let the potatoes marinate.

3. Slice the cucumbers and the radishes into rounds, combine with the potatoes, and sprinkle with finely chopped green onions.

To make the salad taste even better, add a bit of crushed nuts, e.g. walnuts.

21

Bean and pickled onion salad

Ingredients

100 g (3½ oz) red beans

1 red onion

1 tsp powdered sugar

2 cloves garlic

1/2 hot pepper

2 tbsp unrefined oil

1 tbsp apple cider vinegar

Salt

Chopped dill

1. Soak the beans overnight or for 5–6 hours.

2. On the next day, boil the beans in a large amount of water until they are cooked through.

3. Make the dressing. Mix vinegar, oil, powdered sugar, salt, chopped garlic, and dill.

4. Cut the onion in half-moon slices. Combine the beans with the dressing, chopped hot pepper, and the onion.

Autumn salad

Ingredients

- **1 small apple**
- **300 g (10½ oz) red cabbage**
- **80 g (3 oz) carrots**
- **120 g (4 oz) bell peppers**
- **2 tsp apple cider vinegar**
- **Salt**

1. Finely shred the cabbage. Add salt and vinegar. Squeeze the cabbage lightly with your hands.

2. Cut the apple and the bell peppers into matchsticks. Peel the apple if its skin appears too tough.

3. Mix all the ingredients and serve.

Red cabbage and sour cream salad

Ingredients

- **300 g (10½ oz) red cabbage**
- **2 tsp apple cider vinegar or lemon juice**
- **3–4 tbsp sour cream (20% fat)**
- **Salt**

1. Finely shred the cabbage.

2. Add salt and vinegar or lemon juice. Squeeze with your hands and season with sour cream.

Mukachevo salad

Ingredients

200 g (7 oz) cabbage	**1 tsp sugar**
40 g (1½ oz) canned peas	**1 tsp vinegar**
½ small onion	**1 tbsp unrefined oil**
50 g (1⅔ oz) smoked salo, pork belly, or sausage	**1 tbsp refined oil**
	Green onions
1 egg	**Dill**
	Salt

1. Finely shred the cabbage.

2. Cut the onion in half-moon slices. Mix together with the cabbage. Add salt, sugar, and vinegar. Mix thoroughly and squeeze lightly with your hands. Drizzle with oil and leave for 30 minutes.

3. Cut the salo or the sausage into matchsticks. Fry with 1 tbsp of refined oil.

4. Boil and peel the egg. Cut into small pieces.

5. Combine the smoked meat, eggs and canned peas with the cabbage. Sprinkle with chopped dill and green onions. Mix everything thoroughly.

Liver pâté

500 g (1 lb) chicken liver

80 g (3 oz) salo or pork belly

50 g (1½ oz) butter

1 onion

60 g (2 oz) carrots

20 g (½ oz) parsley root

Salt

Ground black pepper

1. Cut the salo into thin slices and put on a frying pan in a single layer. Melt the fat at a low temperature without flipping. Carefully remove the slices of salo.

2. Use the melted fat to fry the diced onions, carrots, and parsley. Remove all the membranes and connective tissues from the liver and cut it into pieces. Combine the liver with the vegetables. Fry until the liver is cooked through. Season with salt and pepper.

3. Melt and strain the butter.

4. Put the whole mixture 2–3 times through a meat grinder. Add ⅔ of the melted butter. Pack into jars and pour the remaining butter on top.

5. Leave the pâté in a fridge for at least 4–5 hours.

Don't eat the butter on top. It only serves as a preservative for the pâté.

Beef heart stewed with carrots and pickled onions

400 g (14 oz) beef heart

200 g (7 oz) carrots

2 medium-sized onions

4 tbsp oil

2 tbsp apple cider vinegar

1 tsp sugar

½ cup boiling water

Salt

½ tsp allspice

½ tsp peppercorns

1 bay leaf

1 tsp ground black pepper

1. Put the beef heart into cold water, bring to a boil and salt generously. Boil the beef heart over low heat for 3–4 hours until it is cooked through. The heart must be easily pierced with a knife.

2. Slice the onions in thin rings. Put them in a deep bowl or a jar, add vinegar, ½ teaspoon of salt, sugar, allspice, peppercorns, and bay leaf. Add boiling water and cover with a lid.

3. Cut the heart into thin slices. Grate the carrots using the large holes.

4. Heat a frying pan, pour half of the oil, and fry the heart slices a little. Add ½ cup of the water you used to boil the meat, sprinkle with salt and pepper, cover with a lid, and stew over low heat for 15–20 minutes.

5. Fry the carrots over medium heat until tender. Drain the marinade from the onions.

6. Mix together the carrots, the frying oil, and the stewed heart. Arrange the pickled onions on top.

Beans with smoked brisket

Ingredients

200 g (7 oz) dried beans

200 g (7 oz) smoked brisket

20 g (½ oz) lard

2 onions

2 cloves garlic

Green onions

Ground black pepper

1. Soak the beans overnight in cold water. If you don't have so much time, cover the beans with boiling water and leave for 2–3 hours.

2. Fry the smoked brisket without oil. Add lard and diced onions. Fry for 2–3 minutes.

3. Add the beans and fry for another 3–4 minutes. Pour a cup of water and season with salt. Cook over medium heat for 40–60 minutes until the beans are cooked through. Stir and add small amounts of water from time to time.

4. Once the beans are cooked, add chopped garlic and black pepper. Remove from the heat, mix thoroughly, and leave for 15 minutes with the lid on.

5. Season with chopped green onions before serving.

Herring and apple appetizer

Ingredients

2 eggs

½ red onion

140 g (5 oz) pickled herring

100 g (3½ oz) apples

Green onion

2 tsp apple cider vinegar

2 tbsp unrefined oil

⅓ tsp ground black pepper

⅓ tsp powdered sugar

1. Make hard-boiled eggs and peel.

2. Finely chop the red onion. Peel the apples.

3. Make the dressing. Combine the powdered sugar, black pepper, vinegar, and oil.

4. Dice the apples, eggs, and herring in uniform pieces. Mix together with the onions and add the dressing.

5. Sprinkle with finely chopped green onions.

Herring on toast with beet

Ingredients

12 slices of brown bread

400 g (14 oz) herring

2 apples

2 beets

1 medium-sized red onion

3–4 tbsp thick sour cream

Dill

1 tsp black brown sugar

1 tbsp apple cider vinegar

1 tbsp unrefined oil

3 tbsp water

1 tsp powdered sugar

1. Boil the beets with the skin on until tender. Leave to cool.

2. Skin and debone the herring. Cut into pieces.

3. Finely chop the dill. Slice the onion into rings. Combine the dill with the onions, ground black pepper, powdered sugar, oil, water, and vinegar. Leave for 1 hour.

4. Grate the apples and the beets using the large holes. Don't add salt. Add the sour cream and mix thoroughly.

5. Slice the bread. Remove the crust and toast the bread on both sides without oil so that the middle remains a bit soft.

6. Drain the marinade from the herring. Leave the onions. Put the beet and apple mixture on the toast. Put a piece of herring and some pickled onions on top. Garnish with dill or green onions.

Eggplant and brynza appetizer

Ingredients

1 eggplant

250 g (9 oz) soft brynza (or any other soft fresh cheese, e.g. ricotta)

1 tomato

Dill and parsley

1 clove garlic

⅓ tsp ground black pepper

1 tbsp oil

Salt

1. Thinly slice the eggplant lengthwise. Sprinkle with salt and leave for 15 minutes. Dab with kitchen tissue and fry with little oil on both sides.

2. Finely chop the greens. Mash the brynza with a fork. Add half of the chopped greens.

3. Plunge the tomato into boiling water from a kettle and leave for one minute. Remove the skin and the seeds. Dice into small cubes. Combine with the squeezed garlic, oil, salt, black pepper, and the remaining greens.

4. Put 1 tablespoon of brynza on a slice of eggplant. Roll them up and put into a deep container so that the rolls lie snugly. Top with the tomatoes.

Salo with garlic

Ingredients

300 g (10½ oz) salo or pork belly

3 cloves garlic

⅓ tsp salt

Black pepper and greens to taste

1. For this appetizer salo should be exceptionally fresh, soft, and with thin skin. Choose a piece which is not very thick.

2. Trim off the skin. Cut the salo into pieces. Mince in a blender or a meat grinder.

3. Squeeze the garlic and stir it into the salo. Season with salt and pepper. Mix thoroughly or use a blender. Taste to check if it needs more salt.

4. If you like, you can also add some chopped dill.

5. Serve with rye bread.

Crackling appetizer

Ingredients

250 g (9 oz) pork belly

1 onion

1. Chop the meat and put it through a meat grinder.

2. Put the meat on a cold frying pan and spread evenly. Melt the fat over medium heat, stirring regularly.

3. Peel the onion and grate using small holes. Squeeze out the juice.

4. Once the cracklings get crispy, add the onion and fry until it becomes golden-brown. Season with salt if the meat is not salted.

5. Put the cracklings into a jar and pour fat on top. Stir when the mixture gets a little solid.

6. Serve with a slice of rye bread and green onions.

Benderyky

It is a delicious dish which resembles chebureky (a national dish of Crimean Tatar cuisine). You can add cilantro or parsley to the minced meat, or add more spices to make it hotter.

Ingredients

200 g (7 oz) minced meat (pork + beef)

½ onion

1 clove garlic

4 eggs

Salt

Ground black pepper

120 g (4 oz) flour

200 ml (1 cup or 7 fl oz) milk 2.5% fat

80 ml (⅓ cup or 2½ fl oz) water

1½ tbsp butter

1 tsp sugar

¼ tsp salt

1. Whisk two eggs with sugar and salt. Add flour and mix thoroughly. Add half of the milk, mix again, and add the remaining milk and water. Add 1½ tablespoons of melted butter (but not too hot). Stir the mixture with a ladle. Scoop and pour the mixture back into the bowl from higher up. This will aerate the batter.

2. Fry pancakes on a cast iron frying pan. Grease the pan with oil every other time, using a cooking brush or a halved potato pierced on a fork.

3. Stack the pancakes and cover with a lid.

4. Peel and grate the onion using small holes. Squeeze out the juice, combine with minced meat, squeezed garlic, salt, and pepper.

5. Cut the pancake in half. Place with the brown side up and put 1 teaspoon of minced meat in the middle. Roll up to make a triangle. Don't put too much meat and spread evenly so that it cooks faster.

6. Whisk the remaining two eggs with salt.

7. Heat a frying pan with oil. Dip benderyky into the egg mixture and deep-fry over low heat with the lid on.

Pancakes with giblets

Ingredients

2 eggs

100 g (3½ oz) flour

150 g (5⅓ oz) milk

1 tsp sugar

1½ tbsp butter

100 ml (½ cup or 3½ fl oz) water

500 g (1 lb) chicken giblets

1 onion

100 g (3½ oz) cream 25% fat

Oil

1. Whisk the eggs with sugar and salt. Add the flour and milk. Mix thoroughly. Add water and 1 tablespoon of melted butter (but not too hot).

2. Clean the chicken hearts from the fat and cut in half. Remove the membranes from the gizzards, wash, and cut into four parts. Cover with cold water and cook until tender.

3. Peel the onion and chop finely. Fry with oil until translucent. Add the boiled hearts and the gizzards. After that, add the liver and fry until half cooked. Pour in the cream.

4. Season with salt and pepper. Reduce the heat. Simmer until the sauce thickens. Add ½ tablespoon of butter in the end.

5. Serve 2 tablespoons of giblets with 2–3 pancakes folded four times.

Zucchini fritters

These fritters can be made lean and without eggs. In this case, you should just add 1 teaspoon of potato starch.

Ingredients

1 zucchini	⅓ bunch dill
1 egg	Salt
1 tbsp flour	Oil
1 clove garlic	

1. Finely grate the zucchini. Sprinkle with salt, leave for 5 minutes, and squeeze out the juice.

2. Add chopped garlic, finely cut dill, egg, and flour.

3. Heat a frying pan with oil. Spoon the mixture into the frying pan and fry on both sides over medium heat.

4. Serve with sour cream.

Fried cauliflower

Ingredients

400 g (14 oz) cauliflower	4 tbsp flour
	Salt
2 eggs	2 cloves garlic

1. Cut the cauliflower into florets, wash thoroughly, and make sure there are no caterpillars. Bring the water to a boil and sprinkle generously with salt. Dunk the cauliflower into the boiling water and cook for 6–8 minutes. The cauliflower should remain a little crispy. Check by piercing a stem with a toothpick.

2. Use a skimmer to put the cauliflower on a plate. Leave to cool.

3. Whisk the egg with salt.

4. Dip the cauliflower first into the egg mixture and then dredge in flour. Fry on all sides with a lot of oil. Turn each floret separately and make sure you fry it on 3–4 sides.

5. Put the fried cauliflower into a bowl, sprinkle with squeezed garlic and toss.

Banosh

Make sure that the sour cream you are going to use for banosh is not too sour. Otherwise you'd better use 20% fat cream. Add corn grits slowly and stir constantly. If there seems to be too much corn, add more milk. It's better to choose pork belly with several layers of meat. As for brynza, it can be made from sheep's milk.

Ingredients

100 g (3½ oz) corn grits

250 g (9 oz) sour cream

300 ml (1 cup or 10 fl oz) milk

100 ml (½ cup or 3½ fl oz) water

250 g (9 oz) pork belly with meat layers

1 onion

250 g (9 oz) brynza (or any other soft fresh cheese, e.g. ricotta)

40 g (1½ oz) butter

Salt

1. Pour the water into a pot and bring to a boil. Add the milk, sour cream, and salt. Again bring to a boil. Stir.

2. Add corn grits and cook until done for about 15 minutes over low heat, stirring constantly. If there appears to be too little liquid, add a little milk or water.

3. Once the banosh is cooked, add the butter. Remove from fire and mix vigorously with a wooden spoon.

4. Slice the meat and fry without oil. Once fat gets melted and the cracklings become slightly crispy, add chopped onion and fry until it becomes golden-brown.

5. Mash the brynza with a fork or use a meat grinder if it is too hard. But it is always better to use fresh and juicy brynza with a buttery taste.

6. Plate up the banosh. Garnish with cracklings and brynza.

Soups, borscht, yushka

Green borscht with chicken

Ingredients

½ medium-sized chicken

2 potatoes

1 carrot

1 onion

3 bunch sorrel

2 eggs

Parsley root

1 tsp peppercorns

2 tbsp oil

1 tbsp butter

2½ L (10½ cups or 5⅓ pt) water

Sour cream

1. Cut the chicken into pieces, cover with water, and bring to the boil. Skim the foam, add salt and pepper, and simmer over low heat until the chicken is cooked through (approximately 2½–3 hours).

2. Peel the vegetables. Dice the onion, grate the parsley root and the carrot, and fry them with a mixture of oil and butter until the vegetables become translucent. Put into the stock.

3. Peel the potatoes, cut, and put into the stock.

4. Sort out the fresh sorrel, cut off the hard stems, wash thoroughly, and chop.

5. Once the potatoes are cooked through, add the sorrel and season with salt. Boil for 2 minutes and remove from the heat.

6. Sprinkle with finely-cut green onions and dill.

7. Plate up and serve with half a hard-boiled egg and a tablespoon of sour cream in each bowl.

Classic borscht

Ingredients

700 g (1½ lb) beef chuck or ribs

20 g (½ oz) lard

1 beet

300 g (10½ oz) cabbage

2–3 potatoes

1 carrot

1 onion

2 cloves garlic

1 tbsp tomato paste or 1 cup of minced tomatoes

1 bay leaf

Ground black pepper

Salt

Sour cream

1. Put the meat into cold water, bring to the boil, and cook over low heat until the beef becomes tender. Take out the meat and put aside.

2. Peel the beet, cut into matchsticks, sprinkle with vinegar, and fry a little. Add the tomato paste and a little water. Simmer until half cooked.

3. Finely chop the onion, julienne the carrot, and fry with lard.

4. Peel the potatoes and cut them into large pieces. Put the potatoes into the meat stock, bring to the boil, and add the shredded cabbage. Boil for 10 minutes.

5. Add the simmered beet, carrot, and onion. Boil until the vegetables are cooked through, but make sure you don't overcook the potatoes and the cabbage. If the cabbage is young and takes less time to cook, add it later.

6. In the end, add the chopped meat, salt, black pepper, bay leaf, and crushed garlic. If the beet is not sweet, you can add 1–2 teaspoons of sugar.

7. Serve with sour cream.

Rooster borscht with beans

Borscht made from a rooster is very tasty and nourishing. Bell peppers and fresh tomatoes add sweetness to the dish. To preserve the vivid color of the beet, you should fry and stew it until half-cooked before putting it into the meat stock. Borscht is cooked over very low heat. Make sure it doesn't boil, but only simmers. Borscht is served with squeezed garlic.

1. Soak the beans overnight or for 6–8 hours. Afterwards, boil until they are cooked through. Make sure that the beans don't pop.

2. Cut the rooster — quarter the breast and cut each leg into three pieces. Cover with cold water and bring to a boil. Skim the foam, and reduce the heat. Allow the stock to simmer for 3–4 hours until the meat becomes tender. Rooster may take from 2 to 5 hours to cook.

3. Cut the beet and the carrots into matchsticks. Peel the potatoes and cut them into 4–6 pieces. Put the potatoes into cold water. Dice the onion, shred the cabbage, and julienne the pepper. Plunge the tomatoes into boiling water from a kettle for one minute, remove the skin, and put through a meat grinder. If the tomatoes are not in season, or if they don't seem to be very tasty, you'd better use tomato paste instead (about 2 tablespoons).

4. Heat the frying pan with 2 tablespoons of oil. Fry the beet over medium heat, add a little boiling water, and stew for 15 minutes, adding more water if necessary.

5. Put the potatoes and the bell pepper into the borscht. Add the beet. If the cabbage is not very young, add it 5 minutes later. If it is young and takes less time to cook, add it 5 minutes before the dish is ready.

6. Take the same frying pan where you've fried the beet. Add another 2–3 tablespoons of oil and fry the carrots together with the onion. Make sure that they don't get burnt.

7. Pour the minced tomatoes into the frying pan, simmer for 5 minutes, and add to the borscht.

8. Once the potatoes are almost cooked, add the beans. Season with salt and pepper.

9. Season with crushed garlic before removing the borscht from the heat. Cover with a lid and leave for a while.

10. Serve with sour cream.

Ingredients

1 rooster

5 potatoes

2 carrots

1 beet

2 onions

8 big ripe tomatoes

1 bell pepper

150 g (5⅓ oz) dried white beans

1 medium-sized cabbage

3 bay leaves

2 cloves garlic

Salt

Ground black pepper

Oil

5 L (21 cups or 1⅓ gal) water

If you like sour borscht, add a spoonful of vinegar at the very end. If you like it sweet, add a spoonful of sugar.

Bograch, or Polonyna soup

Ingredients

500 g (1 lb) beef

70 g (2½ oz) lard

150 g (5⅓ oz) carrots

100 g (3½ oz) parsley root

3 big juicy tomatoes

350 g (12 oz) potatoes

2 onions

400 g (14 oz) bell peppers

2 tbsp dried paprika

1 tsp caraway

2 cloves garlic

Several pieces of hot pepper

Salt

Parsley

1. Melt the lard in a pot with thick sides. Chop the onion and the meat into small pieces and fry them in the melted lard. Add dried paprika. Stew over low heat.

2. Grate the carrots and the parsley root. Add to the meat and pour in a cup of water.

3. Cover the tomatoes with boiling water and leave for 1–2 minutes. Take the tomatoes out of the water and remove the skin. Cut the tomatoes into small cubes and put them into the soup together with the hot pepper.

4. When the meat is almost done, add about 1 liter (4 cups or 2 pt) of water. Bograch is supposed to be a thick soup, so you should probably add small portions of water at a time to control the thickness.

5. Add diced potatoes and season with salt. Boil until the potatoes are cooked through.

6. Use a mortar to grind the caraway and garlic. Add them to the soup at the very end.

7. You can serve bograch with sour cream and garnish with parsley.

Sometimes bograch is served with halushky or chipetke (types of dumplings).

Pea yushka with smoked ribs

Ingredients

300 g (10½ oz) dried peas

500 g (1 lb) smoked ribs

100 g (3½ oz) smoked ham or any other smoked meat

2 onions

1 carrot

1 parsnip root

1½ L (6 cups or 3 pt) water

Oil

Salt

Peppercorns

Allspice

1. Soak the dried peas for 5–6 hours.

2. Take the ribs and the other smoked meat in one piece and cover with water. Bring to a boil and cook for 1–1½ minutes over low heat. Remove the meat from the stock and put aside.

3. Thoroughly rinse the soaked peas and add them to the stock. Skim the foam when it starts boiling.

4. Chop the onions. Finely grate the parsnip and the carrot. Fry them with oil together with the chopped onions. Put into the soup and season with peppercorns and allspice. Add salt if necessary, although smoked meat is usually salty enough.

5. Separate the meat from the bones, cut the smoked meat into pieces, and put into the soup. Cook until the peas are done. Pour in more water if it seems necessary.

6. Sprinkle with finely chopped parsley and serve.

Kapusniak — cabbage soup

This simple and surprisingly tasty cabbage soup can easily compete with borscht!

1. Put the meat into a pot, cover with cold water, and cook over medium heat. Once the water starts to boil, skim the foam, reduce the temperature, and add one whole onion, bay leaf, and several peppercorns. Cover with a lidand cook for 1–1½ hours. Take out the meat and leave to cool. Throw away the cooked onion.

2. Squeeze the brine from the sauerkraut, put into a frying pan, and stew with oil. Put the sauerkraut into the stock and cook for 20 minutes.

3. Wash the millet and soak in very hot water for 15 minutes to reduce the bitterness. Put into the stock and boil for 10 minutes.

4. Wash and peel the potatoes. Cut into medium-sized pieces. Put into the stock and cook for 10 minutes.

5. Chop the onion. Peel the carrot and grate using large holes. Heat a frying pan with oil and fry the onion until golden-brown. Add the carrot, stir, and fry for another 5 minutes. Stir in the tomato paste mixed with water (½ cup of water per 2 tablespoons of paste). Bring to a boil, stirring constantly. Put the vegetables into the soup and simmer for 20 minutes.

6. Cut the meat into pieces and put into the soup. Sprinkle with chopped greens. Season with salt. Cook for another 10 minutes.

7. Serve with sour cream.

Ingredients

- 300 g (10½ oz) beef
- 4 L (17 cups or 1 gal) water
- 4 potatoes
- 1 carrot
- 300 g (10½ oz) sauerkraut
- 2 onions
- 4 tbsp oil
- 2 tbsp millet
- 2 tbsp tomato paste
- Salt
- 1 bay leaf
- Peppercorns
- Greens
- Sour cream

Verkhovyna bean soup

Ingredients

100 g (3½ oz) dried beans

500 g (1 lb) sauerkraut

1 onion

100 g (3½ oz) smoked sausage

100 g (3½ oz) smoked salo (or pork belly)

500 g (1 lb) beef brisket

3 potatoes

1 carrot

100 g (3½ oz) bell peppers

2 fresh tomatoes

½ parsley root

1 tsp peppercorns

1 tsp allspice

2 bay leaves

2 cloves garlic

3½ L (15 cups or 7.4 pt) water

Oil

1. Soak the beans for 5–6 hours. Boil until done.

2. Cover the beef with cold water and bring to a boil. Add the peppercorns, allspice, and bay leaves. Simmer over very low heat until the meat becomes tender. Take out the beef, separate the meat from the bones, and cut into cubes. Strain the stock.

3. Cut the sauerkraut so it will be easier to eat in the soup. Simmer over low heat with little water for 20–25 minutes until the sauerkraut becomes tender.

4. Cut the sausage and the smoked salo into matchsticks and fry. Put into the stock together with the chopped potatoes.

5. Pour boiling water over the tomatoes and leave for 1 minute. Remove the skin and cut into small cubes.

6. Finely grate the parsley root. Dice the carrot, the onion, and the bell peppers. Fry all the vegetables with oil. Add the tomatoes and stew for 3 minutes. Put the vegetables into the stock together with the sauerkraut, the beans, and the beef. Boil until the potatoes are cooked through. Add salt to taste. Season with crushed garlic at the very end.

7. Sprinkle with finely chopped parsley and serve.

Bean soup with smoked meat

This soup takes about 1½ hours to cook. Usually it is enough for the beans to cook through without getting overcooked. If you are not sure, boil the ribs together with the beans until both ingredients are done. After that, take out the beans and put them back at the very end.

Ingredients

100 g (3½ oz) various dried beans

3 potatoes

1 carrot

2 onions

1 hot pepper

4 tomatoes

500 g (1 lb) smoked ribs

100 g (3½ oz) smoked brisket

2 tbsp flour

½ parsley root

Green onions

1. Soak the beans for 5–6 hours.

2. Take the ribs and the brisket in one piece and put them into a pot. Put the beans into the pot as well, cover with water and cook for 1 hour.

3. When the ribs become tender, take out the meat, leave to cool a little, separate the meat from the bones and cut into pieces together with the brisket.

4. Peel the carrot and slice it into rounds. Finely grate the parsley root. Cut the hot pepper into very thin rings. Combine the vegetables and the beans.

5. Pour boiling water over the tomatoes and leave for 1 minute. Remove the skin and cut into cubes. Peel the potatoes and cut them into very large pieces. Put into the soup together with the tomatoes.

6. Finely dice the onion and fry with oil over low heat until the onion becomes tender. Add the flour and stir thoroughly. Add ½ cup of water and stir to prevent lumps. Put into the boiling soup when the potatoes are almost done. Stir, turn down the heat, and boil for another 5 minutes. Season with salt if necessary. Be careful since the smoked meat is usually salty enough.

7. Serve with finely chopped green onions and sour cream.

Goulash

This soup can be made not only with beef, but also with pork or lamb. Choose a piece of meat without bones and make sure it is not too lean. It is better to use meat with a lot of connective tissues (e.g. shanks).

Ingredients

500 g (1 lb) beef

2 onions

150 g (5⅓ oz) bell peppers

3 tsp ground paprika

300 g (10½ oz) potatoes

3 fresh tomatoes

30 g (1 oz) lard

2 cloves garlic

1 tsp ground black pepper

1 pinch caraway

Salt

Water

Parsley

1. Cut the meat into chunks measuring approximately 2 x 2 cm (1 x 1 in). Melt the lard in a pot with thick sides. Add the diced onions and ground paprika. Fry over medium heat for 3–4 minutes. Add a cup of water and simmer for 30–40 minutes.

2. Cover the tomatoes with boiling water and leave for 1 minute. Take the tomatoes out of the water and remove the skin. Chop the tomatoes and the bell peppers. Put into the soup together with the ground caraway and crushed garlic. Season with salt. Cover with a lid and simmer over low heat. Add water if necessary.

3. When the meat is almost done, add about 1 liter (4 cups or 2 pt) of water. The soup is supposed to be very thick.

4. Dice the potatoes and put them into the soup. Boil until the potatoes are cooked through. Season with black pepper.

5. Garnish with parsley.

Mushroom yushka

To make the soup taste even better, you can add a few porcini mushrooms and cook them together with portobello mushrooms. This will guarantee a delicious smell.

Ingredients

400 g (14 oz) portobello mushrooms and 2–3 mushrooms for garnish

4 tbsp cream 20% fat

2 tbsp butter

1 onion

Ground black pepper

Salt

1. Thinly slice the mushrooms. Grate the onion using small holes.

2. Melt ⅔ of the butter in a deep frying pan. Use it to fry the onion over low heat for 3–4 minutes. Season with salt and add the mushrooms. Cook for 7–10 minutes until the mushrooms become tender. If the mushrooms release too much moisture, turn up the heat to evaporate the liquid.

3. Reduce the heat again. Add one tablespoon of cream at a time. Wait until the cream thickens before adding another spoon.

4. Turn up the heat and pour in water (about 600 ml / 2½ cups / 1 pt). Make sure that the soup remains thick, so it's better to add water in small portions.

5. Cook for 5–6 minutes. Stir in the remaining butter, whisk with a wooden spoon, and remove from the heat. Butter will prevent the soup from getting layered.

6. Garnish the soup with fried portobello mushrooms, parsley, and ground black pepper.

You can turn this dish into a tasty puréed soup if you blend it in a blender.

Fish yushka

Ingredients

1 zander	½ tsp peppercorns
2 onions	½ tsp allspice
2 carrots	2½ L (10½ cups or 5⅓ pt) water
4 potatoes	
2 bay leaves	

1. Scale the fish, remove the fins and the gills. Cut off the head. Separate the meat from the bones.

2. Cover the bones and the head with water and bring to a boil. Add peeled carrots, onions, bay leaves, peppercorns, and allspice. Reduce the heat and cook for 1 hour. Strain the stock.

3. Peel the potatoes and cut into large pieces. Put into the stock and boil until half cooked. Add chopped meat and carrots. Boil until the potatoes are cooked through. Season with salt and chopped parsley.

Green pea yushka

Ingredients

200 g (7 oz) green peas (frozen peas are fine)	2 tbsp butter
	2 stalks of green onion
6 pieces of smoked salo (or pork belly)	500 ml (2 cups or 1 pt) water
	Salt

1. Melt the butter in a pot, add the peas, and simmer over medium heat for 7–10 minutes, stirring regularly.

2. Finely cut the green onions together with the white parts. Add to the peas, season with salt, and fry for another 3 minutes. Use a potato masher to slightly mash the peas.

3. Add 500 ml (2 cups or 1 pt) of water and cook for several minutes. Season with salt. If the soup appears too thick, add more water. Bring to a boil and remove from the heat.

4. Place the pieces of salo on a frying pan in a single layer. Heat to melt out the fat until the salo becomes golden-yellow.

5. Serve the soup immediately with salo and green onions.

You can also blend this soup to make a delicious purée.

Potato yushka

Smooth texture and buttery taste! This soup is best served with croutons.

Ingredients

200 g (7 oz) onions

200 g (7 oz) potatoes

50 g (1⅔ oz) butter

40 ml (3 tbsp) milk 3.2% fat

20 ml (1½ tbsp) cream

100 ml (½ cup or 3½ fl oz) water

5 g (0.2 oz) parsnip

A sprig of parsley

1. Grate the onion using the smallest holes.

2. Cut the potatoes and rinse with cold running water to remove extra starch. Leave in water for 2 minutes.

3. Melt ½ of the butter in a deep frying pan or in a heavy-bottomed pot. Add the onions and simmer over low heat for 5 minutes. Don't let the onions become brown. Add the potatoes, grated parsnip, and a sprig of parsley. Mix thoroughly. Add water in small portions if necessary to prevent the potatoes from sticking to the bottom.

4. Cook the soup, stirring regularly and breaking any lumps with a spoon. At the very end mash it with a masher until smooth.

5. Once the potatoes are cooked through and the smell of raw onion goes away, take out the parsley. Add salt, milk, and cream. Boil for a short time and add water. The soup should not be very thick, so add only a small amount of water at a time. Add the butter in the end.

6. To achieve a smooth texture, pass the soup through a sieve or use a blender.

7. Garnish with green onions and croutons made of white bread.

Ohirchanka with kidneys

Ingredients

2 beef kidneys

4 pickled cucumbers

2 potatoes

1 onion

½ parsley root

½ carrot

⅙ celery root

100 g (3½ oz) rice

Bay leaves

Chopped parsley and dill

1 L (4 cups or 2 pt) beef stock

Pickle brine

Oil

Peppercorns

1. Cut the kidneys in half lengthwise. Remove the fat and the veins. Put into a bowl and pour in cold water with 1 tablespoon of salt. Leave for 1–2 hours.

2. Drain the kidneys and pour in new water. Bring to a boil and cook for 10 minutes. Drain and repeat the procedure one more time. Cook until tender. Take out the kidneys and dice into small cubes.

3. Finely grate the celery, parsley root, and carrot. Fry with oil. Put into the boiling stock together with bay leaves and peppercorns.

4. Peel the pickled cucumbers. If the seeds are big, remove them as well. Dice the pickles and the onion.

5. Boil the rice until half cooked.

6. Fry the onion with oil. Add the pickles, simmer, and put into the stock. Cook for 40 minutes.

7. Peel the potatoes, cut into pieces, and put into the soup. When the potatoes are almost done, add the kidneys and rice. Boil until the potatoes are cooked through. If the soup is not salty enough, add a little brine.

8. Sprinkle with finely-chopped parsley and dill before serving. The soup tastes good with sour cream, too.

Krupnyk

Ingredients

200 g (7 oz) pearl barley

Giblets from 3 chickens

40 g (1½ oz) carrot

1 onion

8 pieces of dried porcini mushrooms

150 g (5⅓ oz) potatoes

40 g (1½ oz) butter

1 tbsp oil

2 L (8½ cups or ½ gal) water

1. Soak the barley in cold water overnight. If you don't have so much time, cover with boiling water and leave for 4 hours.

2. Cover the porcini mushrooms with water and leave for 2–3 hours.

3. Rince the barley and cover with 2 cm (1 in) of water above the surface. Cook for about 40 minutes until done. Stir in the butter and keep stirring with a wooden spoon until the barley turns white. Season with salt.

4. Remove all the membranes from the liver and cut into pieces. Clean the chicken hearts from the fat, remove the membranes from the gizzards, and cut into 2 parts.

5. Pour water over the chicken necks, wings, gizzards, and hearts. Cook over very low heat for about an hour until done. Strain the stock and remove the meat.

6. Dice the onion and the carrot. Fry with oil. Drain the mushrooms and mix together with the vegetables. Simmer a little and then put into the stock. Cook over low heat for 30 minutes.

7. Peel the potatoes and cut them into pieces. Put into the stock.

8. Separate the meat from the bones. Add the chicken meat, gizzards, hearts, and liver 5 minutes before the potatoes are cooked through. Add the cooked barley in the end. Season with salt if necessary.

9. Garnish with parsley.

Raftsmen's soup

Ingredients

400 g (14 oz) lamb

60 g (2 oz) lard

1 onion

5 potatoes

400 g (14 oz) green beans

3½ L (15 cups or 7.4 pt) water

½ tsp caraway

Salt

Ground black pepper

1. Cut the meat into small pieces and fry in a pot with thick sides. Add finely chopped onion, ground caraway, and black pepper.

2. Pour in a cup of boiling water and stew over low heat for 40–60 minutes until the meat becomes tender. Add more water if necessary, but make sure you stew the meat rather than boil.

3. Pour in the remaining water and bring to a boil.

4. Peel the potatoes, cut into medium-sized pieces, and put into the stock. Boil until the potatoes are half-cooked and add the beans. Season with salt and boil until cooked through.

5. Sprinkle with finely chopped parsley and serve.

Pumpkin soup

Ingredients

600 g (1⅓ lb) pumpkin

30 g (1 oz) butter

200 ml (1 cup or 7 fl oz) water

100 ml (½ cup or 3½ fl oz) milk 3.2% fat

100 g (3½ oz) shelled pumpkin seeds

3–4 slices of white bread

2 onions

1. Finely grate the onion using small holes. Fry over low heat for 5 minutes, making sure that the onion doesn't get brown.

2. When the smell of the raw onion goes away, add the pumpkin and cook for another 10 minutes without turning up the heat.

3. Add water and boil for 20 minutes. Season with salt. Pour in the milk and cook for another 10 minutes.

4. Remove the soup from the heat and pass through a sieve.

5. Fry the pumpkin seeds without oil for 5 minutes, stirring constantly.

6. Slice the bread into small triangular pieces and dry in the oven at 190 °C (375 °F) for 20–25 minutes.

7. Plate up and garnish with pumpkin seeds and croutons.

Kholodnyk

Ingredients

3 potatoes

1 cucumber

1 beet

3 eggs

250 g (9 oz) sour cream 25% fat

Green onions

Dill

1 lemon

1 tbsp powdered sugar

Salt

1½ L (6 cups or 3 pt) water

1. Peel the beet, cover with water, and cook for 40–60 minutes until done. Take out the beet and put aside. Pour lemon juice into the broth, add salt and sugar. Taste and add more if necessary.

2. Boil the potatoes in jackets. Make hard boiled eggs.

3. Cut the beet into matchsticks or grate using large holes.

4. Dice the cucumber, peeled eggs, and potatoes in uniform pieces. Pour in the broth. Add sour cream and chopped greens.

5. Serve it very cold.

Okroshka

Ingredients

3 potatoes

2 cucumbers

200 g (7 oz) beef

¼ chicken

3 eggs

1 tbsp mustard

1 lemon

300 g (10½ oz) sour cream

1 tbsp peppercorns

1 onion

1 bunch green onions

1 bunch dill

1½–2 L (2 pt–½ gal) water

1. Cover the beef and the chicken with water and bring to the boil. Skim the foam and add peppercorns and onion. Simmer for 3–3½ hours until the meat starts falling off the bones.

2. Boil the potatoes with skin. Make hard boiled eggs.

3. Take out the meat and leave to cool. Strain the stock. Peel the eggs and the potatoes. Taste the cucumber. If the skin is bitter and thick, peel them.

4. Put the yolks aside. Dice the egg whites, potatoes, cucumbers, and meat in uniform pieces. Put into a pot.

5. Stir the yolks in a bowl with salt, mustard, lemon juice, and finely chopped greens. Mix with sour cream and room temperature stock. Stir until smooth. Pour this mixture over the vegetables and meat. Taste and add more salt, mustard, and lemon juice if necessary. Cover with a lid. Leave in the fridge for 2–3 hours.

Main Dishes

Chicken sausages

Sausages will taste better if you use chicken parts with the highest fat content, such as thighs or drumsticks. If you take lean cuts, add a little salo or pork fat.

Ingredients

600 g (1⅓ lb) fatty chicken parts

2 cloves garlic

Black pepper

Dill

1 m (3⅓ ft) casing

1. Debone the chicken. Remove the skin but save the fat.

2. Put the meat and the garlic through a meat grinder.

3. Finely chop the dill. Mix the minced meat and the dill. Add 8 tablespoons of hot water, approximately 50–60 °C (120–140 °F).

4. Stuff the casing using a special stuffer nozzle on your meat grinder or a funnel made out of a plastic bottle (see the krovianka recipe above). Leave the sausage in the fridge for 1 hour.

5. Pierce the sausages with a needle on both sides about every 3 cm (1 in).

6. Bake on a baking tray in the oven at 190 °C (375 °F) for 40–50 minutes.

Krovianka — blood sausage

This is a classic recipe of black pudding without any cereal, eggs or bread. The blood must be fresh for this recipe.

Ingredients

300 ml (1⅓ cups or 10 fl oz) pork blood

300 g (10½ oz) fat pork (there must be around 30% meat and 70% fat), half of the meat can be replaced with salted salo or pork belly

2 onions

3 cloves garlic

1 tbsp ground black pepper

½ m (1½ ft) sausage casing

1. Mince the salo and the meat in a meat grinder together with the onion (use large holes). Put into a cold frying pan and fry over medium heat.

2. Pass the blood through the meat grinder or through a sieve. You can use a blender instead.

3. Mix the blood with the fried salo and meat. Add chopped garlic, black pepper, and salt.

4. Stuff the casing. In order to do that, use a special stuffer nozzle on your meat grinder or simply use the top part of a plastic bottle. For that, take a clear plastic bottle and cut it crosswise so that the top part resembles a funnel. Pull the casing over the bottleneck and start pushing the meat through with a spoon. Tie the ends of the casing with a string. To be on the safe side, tie a knot on the casing as well.

5. Put your sausage in cold water and bring to a boil. Cook for about 15–20 minutes. Pierce the casing with a needle somewhere in the middle. If the black pudding is ready, the juice will be transparent. Otherwise, cook for another 5–10 minutes.

6. Take out of the water and leave to cool. You can fry the black pudding with salo before serving.

Baked kashanka — blood porridge sausage

Instead of buckwheat, you can use a different type of cereal to make kashanka. For instance, you can use some semolina, but keep in mind that semolina tends to increase in size several times when cooked. Rice, millet, or even white bread will do nicely as well.

Ingredients

400 ml (1¾ cups or 14 fl oz) fresh pork blood

150 g (5⅓ oz) pork belly

100 g (3½ oz) onion

100 g (3½ oz) cooked buckwheat

Salt

1 tbsp ground black pepper

5 cloves garlic

½ m (1½ ft) casing

1. Put the pork belly through a meat grinder together with the onion (use large hole size). Put into a cold frying pan and fry over medium heat.

2. Pass the blood through a meat grinder or through a sieve. You can also use a blender instead.

3. Cook the buckwheat until done and make sure that all the water evaporates.

4. Mix the blood with the fried salo. Add chopped garlic, buckwheat, black pepper, and salt.

5. Stuff the casing in the same way as in the krovianka recipe above.

6. Put the sausage on a greased baking tray. Pierce the casing every 4–5 cm (1½ – 2 in).

7. Bake in the oven at 190 °C (375 °F) for 40–60 minutes.

8. Pierce the sausage in the middle with a needle. If it is ready, the juice will be transparent. Otherwise, bake for another 10–15 minutes.

Pashtetivka — liver sausage

Ingredients

500 g (1 lb) beef liver

1 onion

1 clove garlic

80 g (3 oz) butter

200 g (7 oz) salo

1–1½ tsp salt

Ground black pepper

1 m (3⅓ ft) casing

1. Cut the liver into big pieces — about 4 x 4 cm (1½ x 1½ in). Put into boiling water and cook for 10–15 minutes until done. Take out the liver and leave to cool a little. Membranes can be easily removed when the liver is warm.

2. Remove all the membranes and put the liver through a meat grinder (use the smallest holes) together with the onion and the garlic. Put the salo through the meat grinder as well (use large holes) or chop it finely with a knife. Mix everything together.

3. Add melted butter, salt, and pepper to taste. Pour in 7–9 tablespoons of hot water. Mix thoroughly.

4. Stuff the casing using a special stuffer nozzle on your meat grinder or a funnel made out of a plastic bottle (see the krovianka recipe above). Leave the sausage in the fridge for 1 hour.

5. Put the sausage into cold water, bring to a boil and cook for 10 minutes. Make sure that the water doesn't boil.

6. Take out the sausage and leave to cool.

7. Serve with croutons, butter, and pickled cucumbers.

Homemade sausage

Ingredients

600 g (1⅓ lb) pork neck

180 g (6⅓ oz) pork belly

2 cloves garlic

8 tbsp warm water

1 tbsp allspice

1 tbsp peppercorn

1 tbsp ground paprika

1–1½ tsp salt

½ tsp red hot pepper

1. Finely slice half of the pork neck. Put the other half through a meat grinder together with the pork belly, allspice, and garlic. Add hot pepper, paprika, salt, and water. Mix together with the sliced meat.

2. Stuff the casing using a special stuffer nozzle on your meat grinder or a funnel made out of a plastic bottle (see the blood pudding recipe above). Don't stuff too tightly. Tie the knots on both ends and leave the sausage in the fridge for 1 hour.

3. Take a baking tray and grease it with lard or some other fat. Pierce the sausage on both sides every 3 cm (1 in) and cook in the oven at 190 °C (375 °F) for about 40–50 minutes until done. Baste with fat every 10–15 minutes.

Homemade stew

Ingredients

400 g (14 oz) pork neck

2 tbsp lard

600 g (1⅓ lb) potatoes

1 carrot

3 onions

Allspice

Peppercorns

Bay leaf

Salt

1. Cut the meat into medium-sized pieces. Take a cauldron or any other heavy-bottomed pot with thick sides. Melt the lard in the pot until golden-brown. Add diced onion. Mix and cook for 5 minutes.

2. Peel and cut the carrot. Combine with the meat and season with spices. Pour in half a glass of water and cover with a lid.

3. Peel the potatoes and cut into big chunks. Mix with the meat when it is almost done.

4. Sprinkle with salt. Stew until the potatoes are cooked through. Add water if necessary.

Hodzia — pork and vegetable stew

Hodzia is a thick hot dish made from pork. If the meat you have seems a bit too lean, you can add some pork belly. This dish is convenient to cook for a big company. Besides, you don't have to constantly keep an eye on it while cooking. If you don't have a cauldron, you can cook it in a large baking pan in the oven, but make sure you cover it with a lid.

Ingredients

- **300 g (10½ oz) pork (shoulder, neck or ribs)**
- **5 potatoes**
- **2 onions**
- **1 carrot**
- **600 g (1⅓ lb) cabbage**
- **5 pickled cucumbers (Choose small and firm cucumbers with small seeds. They should taste sweet rather than sour.)**
- **80 g (3 oz) dried beans**
- **1 glass tomato juice**
- **½ tbsp allspice**
- **½ tbsp peppercorns**
- **3 bay leaves**
- **Salt**
- **Water or stock**
- **Oil**

1. Soak the beans overnight. Add 1 liter (4 cups or 2 pt) of water per 80 grams (3 oz) of dried beans. To speed up the process, you can cover the beans with boiling water and leave for 3 hours).

2. Take a cauldron or a heavy-bottomed pot with thick sides. Heat the pot. Chop the meat and fry with oil.

3. Add the soaked beans, cover with a lid, and simmer for 20–25 minutes. Add coarsely diced carrot and onions. Make sure there is no water or meat juice in the cauldron, as you want to fry the vegetable a little rather than boil.

4. Slice the pickles into rounds if they are small. If they are big, cut them in half-moon slices. Put the pickles into the cauldron. Add ½ glass of water. The beans will absorb a lot of water, so keep an eye on the dish and add more water when necessary. Stew for about 1 hour or more depending on the meat and the beans.

5. Cut the potatoes into medium-sized pieces. Shred the cabbage. When the beans are almost done, add the potatoes. Stew for 15 minutes until the potatoes are half cooked. Add the shredded cabbage, bay leaves, salt, allspice, and peppercorns. Pour in the tomato juice. Mix thoroughly.

6. Remove from the heat when the cabbage is still crispy. Keep the lid on for half an hour.

7. Serve hodzia with sour cream and garnish with greens. Just like borscht, it tastes better on the following day.

Honey glazed pork ribs

Ingredients

1 kg (2 lb) pork ribs

70 g (2½ oz) honey

1 tsp sweet pepper powder

½ tsp hot pepper

2 tbsp oil

1 tsp mustard

1 tsp peppercorns

½ tsp allspice

3 bay leaves

1. Chop the ribs. If they are thick, separate each rib with a knife. If the ribs are thin, make chunks consisting of 2–3 ribs each.

2. Put the chopped ribs into the boiling water. Add bay leaves, salt, allspice, and peppercorns. Boil until tender. The meat shouldn't become too soft or fall apart.

3. Leave the ribs to cool without removing them from the stock. If you don't have so much time, take out the ribs and leave them to cool in a different pot. Make sure you cover them with a lid though, to prevent the ribs from getting too dry. A smart way is to boil the ribs one day before cooking the dish.

4. If the honey is very thick, melt it a bit. Mix together the honey, mustard, hot and sweet pepper, and pour in 1 tablespoon of stock. Mix everything thoroughly.

5. Carefully dry the ribs. Pat them with a paper towel.

6. Coat the ribs with the sauce on all sides with a cooking brush. Add 1–2 tablespoons of oil to the remaining sauce. Put aside.

7. Arrange the ribs on a wire rack. Place a baking tray beneath for the dripping fat. Preheat the oven to 190 °C (375 °F). Roast the ribs. In 15–20 minutes, once the sauce creates a glaze on the ribs, baste them with the remaining sauce mixed with oil. Baste every 7–10 minutes and roast until a crispy glaze appears.

Crispy pork knuckles with mustard and honey

Pork knuckles are especially tasty if you season the stock with lots of spices and aromatic roots, such as parsnip, celery, or parsley root. Or you can simply add a carrot and a couple of onions.

Ingredients

1½ kg (3⅓ lb) pork knuckles	4 bay leaves
100 g (3½ oz) honey	1 tbsp peppercorns
1 tbsp mustard	1 big onion
1 tbsp oil	1 carrot
2 heads garlic	Parsnip and parsley roots
1 tbsp allspice	

1. Thoroughly wash the pork knuckles and make sure they are free from bristles. Singe them over the gas if necessary.

2. Put the meat into a big pot with cold water and bring to a boil.

3. Turn down the heat and add salt, one head of garlic, onion, spices, and roots. Taste the stock to check the amount of salt — the stock must be very salty.

4. Cook for about 4 hours until tender. The knuckles should be easily pierced with a knife.

5. It is recommended to cool the meat in the same stock where you have cooked it. A smart way would be to boil the knuckles one day before making the dish. If you don't have so much time, remove the meat from the stock and leave to cool on a plate. Pat dry and put into the cold oven. Heat the oven to 165 °C (325 °F) and cook for 40 minutes.

6. Make the glaze. For that, combine the honey, mustard, and 2 tablespoons of stock. If you like hot food, add 1 teaspoon of hot red pepper.

7. Take the knuckles out of the oven, baste with the glaze, and put back into the oven.

8. Baste the meat every 15–20 minutes with a cooking brush.

9. When the knuckles are almost done and become golden-brown, and you've used up all the glaze, stir 1 head of crushed garlic with 1 tablespoon of oil. Brush the knuckles with this mixture and cook for another 15–20 minutes. Keep an eye on the dish to prevent the garlic from burning.

10. Serve the pork knuckles with horseradish or mustard.

11. Boiled potatoes or stewed sauerkraut with caraway (see p. 87) will make a good side dish for the knuckles.

Lotsi — pork stew with onions

Ingredients

3 big pieces of loin

5 onions

2 cloves garlic

15 g (½ oz) lard

3 tsp ground paprika

Ground black pepper

Salt

Oil

1. Tenderize the meat on all sides. Sprinkle with paprika and black pepper. Fry with oil over high heat until crisp and golden. Put aside.

2. Cut the onions in half-moon slices and fry with lard in the same frying pan. Add crushed garlic and warm.

3. Put the meat on top of the onions, pour in 100 ml (½ cup or 3½ fl oz) of water, turn down the heat and cover with a lid. Stew on one side for 7–10 minutes, then turn and cook for another 7–10 minutes. Add water if necessary. Season with salt.

Pork belly stew

Ingredients

250 g (9 oz) pork belly with thick layers of meat

1 onion

40 g (1½ oz) carrot

100 g (3½ oz) zucchini

120 g (4 oz) bell peppers

40 g (1½ oz) green beans

Ground black pepper

Oil

1. Dice all the vegetables except the green beans. Try to dice the carrot and the onion into smaller cubes.

2. Cut the pork belly and fry without oil. Then pour in a little oil, add chopped carrots and onions, and fry over low heat for 10 minutes. Make sure the vegetables don't get dark.

3. Add the bell peppers and turn up the heat to the medium level. Add the zucchini and the green beans 5–6 minutes before the dish is ready.

4. Season the stew with salt and pepper.

Stewed cabbage with caraway

Ingredients

2 onions	2 tbsp oil
600 g (1⅓ lb) sauerkraut	2 tsp caraway

1. Cut the onion in half-moon slices. Fry over medium heat for 2–3 minutes. Cut the sauerkraut to make it easier to eat. Mix the onion and the sauerkraut. Fry a little, then pour in ½ glass of water and stew for

10 minutes uncovered. Add the caraway, cover with the lid, and cook for 40–50 minutes, adding water from time to time.

Holubtsi in Zakarpattia style — stuffed cabbage leaves

Ingredients

500 g (1 lb) pork neck

1 head cabbage

4 onions

70 g (2½ oz) lard

300 g (10½ oz) fat sour cream

20 g (½ oz) flour

30 g (1 oz) tomato paste

2 cloves garlic

3 bay leaves

½ tsp allspice

Salt

Ground black pepper

1. Cut off the stem of the cabbage or simply cut a notch along the perimeter. Put the cabbage into salted boiling water and cook for 2–4 minutes. Take out the cabbage and remove the outer leaves. Continue removing the leaves one by one until you have nothing but the core left.

2. Use a sharp knife to cut off thick veins on each leaf.

3. Cut the meat in small, thin slices and tenderize them.

4. Dice the onions into small cubes and fry with lard. You will use half of the onions to make the filling for the holubtsi. The other half will be used to make the sauce.

5. Put a slice of meat on a cabbage leaf. Put some fried onions on top and roll the leaf.

6. Line the bottom of your pot with cabbage leaves. Lay the rolls snugly in several layers. Pour in a glass of boiling water and sprinkle with salt. Cover with a lid and stew for 20–25 minutes.

7. In order to make the sauce, take the remaining fried onions, add the tomato paste, bay leaves, allspice, squeezed garlic, and ½ glass of water. Stew over low heat for 5 minutes.

8. Fry the flour without oil. Add the sour cream.

9. Stir the tomato paste into the flour and sour cream mixture. Mix thoroughly and pour this sauce over the rolls. Stew for 20 minutes until the meat and the cabbage become tender.

10. Serve holubtsi with the sauce in which you have stewed the rolls.

Holubtsi in Hutsul style with smoked brisket — stuffed young cabbage leaves

Ingredients

15 leaves of young cabbage

600 g (1⅓ lb) minced meat (beef + pork)

200 g (7 oz) smoked brisket

4 onions

60 g (2 oz) millet

2 carrots

1. Wash the millet thoroughly, cover with boiling water, and leave for 1 hour. Cook for 5 minutes until half done. Drain.

2. If the cabbage is not very tight and firm, remove the leaves from the head. If the leaves are tightly packed, cut out the stem or make a notch along its perimeter and dunk the cabbage head into the boiling water for 1–2 minutes. Remove the loosened cabbage leaves. Repeat with each layer of the cabbage.

3. Chop the brisket into small pieces and cook over very low heat to let the fat melt. Add half of the finely chopped onions. Put the remaining onions aside. You are going to use them for the gravy. Turn up the heat and fry until golden-brown.

4. Mix the fried onions and the brisket with the minced meat and the millet. Season with salt and ground black pepper. Mix thoroughly.

5. If you've managed to take the leaves off the cabbage head without boiling, take a big pot or a deep frying pan, pour in boiling water, and dunk one cabbage leaf at a time for 10–20 seconds to make it soft.

6. Use a sharp knife to cut off thick veins on each leaf. Put 1 tablespoon of the filling in the middle of each leaf. Roll up towards the thick edge of the leaf.

7. Grate the carrots using large holes and fry with oil. Add the remaining onions and fry until translucent.

8. Line the baking tray with cabbage leaves. Lay the rolls snugly. Put the fried carrots and onions on top. Pour a glass of boiling water and cover with cabbage leaves.

9. Preheat the oven to 190 °C (375 °F). Put the cabbage rolls in the oven and cook for 40–60 minutes until the meat is done.

Meat with knedli

Ingredients

For meat:

1 kg (2 lb) pork

1 carrot

1 onion

1 head of garlic

1 tbsp dried mushrooms

1 parsley root

1 tbsp butter

1 tsp peppercorns

½ tsp allspice

½ tsp mustard seeds

1 bay leaf

For knedli:

500 g (1 lb) potatoes

70 g (2½ oz) flour

1 egg

Salt

1. Fry the meat on all sides. Peel the onion, parsley root, and carrot. Wash the garlic and cut off the roots. Fry the vegetables in the same frying pan where you've cooked the meat. Put the meat, vegetables, mushrooms, and spices into a big, heavy-bottomed pot. Pour a glass of water into a frying pan, bring to a boil. Thoroughly scrape everything from the frying pan and pour it over the meat. Cover with a lid and stew. Turn the meat in 30 minutes' time and add some water. In the end, you should end up with approximately a glass full of sauce. Stew until done.

2. Remove the pork and strain the sauce. Mash the vegetables or pass them through a sieve if possible.

3. Mix 1 tablespoon of flour with 2 tablespoons of water. Stir into the boiling sauce and cook until thickened. Remove from the heat, add butter, and mix thoroughly. Put the meat back into the pot.

4. Now make knedli (potato dumplings). Boil the potatoes in jackets. Don't overcook. Make sure the peel doesn't crack. Leave to cool a little so that you can touch the potatoes. Finely grate the potatoes, mix with egg, then add salt and flour. Make the dough and knead for 2–3 minutes. Sprinkle with flour if necessary.

5. Bring a large pot of water to a boil.

6. Make small balls and boil them in salted water until they rise.

7. Cut the meat into pieces. Serve with knedli and sauce.

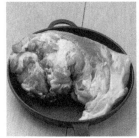    

Pork ribs stewed with cabbage, or Bigos

Ingredients

1½ kg (3⅓ lb) cabbage

½ kg (1 lb) pork ribs

2 onions

1 tbsp tomato paste or ½ glass of freshly minced tomatoes

1 tsp peppercorns

1 tsp allspice

6 bay leaves

Oil

1. Cut the ribs and boil them in salted water together with bay leaves, allspice, and peppercorns. Use half of the spices. The other half will be used for stewing.

2. Take out the ribs and pat them dry.

3. Heat the oil in a big, heavy-bottomed pot. Fry the ribs in the pot. Add chopped onions and spices.

4. Shred the cabbage, squeeze it slightly, salt, and add to the meat. Mix carefully, reduce the heat, and cover with a lid. Stir regularly to prevent the cabbage from sticking.

5. When the cabbage is almost cooked through, add the tomato paste mixed together with 2 tablespoons of stock. Mix thoroughly and stew until done. Taste the cabbage to check the amount of spices. You can also add some sugar or lemon juice.

Kruchenyky in Mukachevo style — minced beef rolls

Ingredients

500 g (1 lb) minced beef

50 g (1⅔ oz) salo (or pork belly)

150 g (5⅓ oz) porcini mushrooms

3 tbsp flour

15 g (½ oz) lard

2 onions

250 g (9 oz) fat sour cream

1 egg

Salt

Ground black pepper

Oil

1. Dice the salo into small cubes. Combine with minced beef, egg, salt, and black pepper. Bash the mince by taking a handful and throwing it back into the bowl from a height 10 times. Leave in the fridge for 30 minutes. Make sausages (kruchenyky) 4 cm (1½ in) in diameter. Dredge in flour and fry with oil on all sides.

2. Make mushroom sauce. Finely chop the onions and fry with lard. Add the diced mushrooms and fry until golden-brown. Season with salt and pepper. Add the sour cream, cook for 2 minutes, and pour in ½ glass of water.

3. Put kruchenyky into a saucepan and cover with the sauce. Stew for 15–20 minutes until thickened.

4. Serve kruchenyky with the mushroom sauce and sprinkle with finely chopped parsley.

Kruchenyky in Khust style — pork rolls

Ingredients

800 g (1¾ lb) pork loin or lean neck

4 onions

150 g (5⅓ oz) smoked salo (or pork belly)

100 g (3½ oz) pickled mushrooms

6 tomatoes

3 tbsp flour

1 tsp sugar

Salt

Black pepper

Oil

1. Peel the onions and chop finely.

2. Cut the pork into thin pieces. Tenderize and sprinkle with salt and pepper.

3. Dice the salo and fry over medium heat. Add half of the onions and fry until tender. Add peeled and diced pickles. Mix everything.

4. Put 1 tablespoon of fried salo and vegetables on a tenderized piece of meat and make a roll (kruchenyk). Dredge in flour and fry on all sides.

5. Make the sauce. Peel the tomatoes and put them through a meat grinder. Fry the remaining onions and mix with the tomato sauce. Add sugar, salt, and black pepper. Then simmer for 15 minutes.

6. Put kruchenyky into a saucepan, cover with the sauce, and stew for 20–25 minutes until done.

Kholodets — aspic or meat jelly

1 beef trotter

1 beef shank

1 kg (2 lb) lean meat

2 carrots

1 parsley root

2 onions

1½ head garlic

4 bay leaves

1 tbsp peppercorns

½ tbsp allspice

Salt

1. Meat from older animals will do better for this dish, rather than from young calves. The shank should be dark and meaty. To make sure the beef shanks will fit into your pot, ask your butcher to chop it when buying. Pork trotters can be used to make kholodets as well, but you will need two pork trotters for this amount of water. Kholodets thickens well with beef tails, heads, and knuckles, too. You can also make kholodets with a rooster, but make sure you add trotters as well.

2. Wash the meat thoroughly, remove small fragments of bones, singe the trotter, and trim it with a knife if necessary.

3. Put all the meat into a big (10 L / 2⅔ gal) pot and cover with water. Make sure you leave some place in the pot for the vegetables.

4. Bring to a boil and turn down the heat. Don't let the stock boil. Don't cover with a lid either. Otherwise, the stock will become turbid and greasy.

5. Peel the carrots and the parsley root. Don't peel the garlic and the onions. Wash thoroughly and trim the roots with a knife. Onion peels will add a beautiful color to the dish. Put the vegetables into the stock.

6. Skim the foam and the grease constantly.

7. In general, it takes about 8 hours to cook kholodets. Season with salt and spices 1½ –2 hours before the stock is ready. At the very end taste it to check the amount of salt. Keep in mind that the stock will taste less salty once it cools down.

8. When the stock cools down a bit, take out the meat and strain the stock through a piece of cheesecloth.

9. Separate the meat into pieces manually in order to feel small bones. Cut with a knife into smaller pieces measuring approximately 2 cm (¾ in). It is ok to add some pieces of skin and soft gristle. Squeeze half of the garlic head, mix it together with the meat, and sprinkle with salt.

10. Distribute the meat into molds. Put some pieces of boiled carrots on top if you like. Cover with 2 cm (¾ in) of stock.

11. Leave to cool at room temperature and then put into the fridge.

12. Serve kholodets with mustard and horseradish when it thickens.

Homemade noodles with meatballs in tomato sauce

Ingredients

For the meatballs:

3 tomatoes

1 onion

½ tsp thyme

1 tsp ground paprika

500 g (1 lb) minced beef

For the noodles:

1 egg

150 g (5⅓ oz) flour

1–2 tbsp water

¼ tsp salt

1. Sift the flour, add salt, and mix. Crack the egg and stir it into the middle. Add a little water and make the dough. Add more water and flour if necessary. Knead the dough for 10–15 minutes until it becomes smooth and elastic. Wrap in cling wrap and leave for 40 minutes.

2. Divide the dough into several pieces. Roll out one piece at a time while keeping the other pieces wrapped in cling wrap to prevent them from getting dry.

3. Dust each piece of dough with some flour and roll it out as thinly as possible. Loosely roll the dough into a spiral and cut it crosswise. Leave the noodles to dry.

4. Season the minced meat with salt and black pepper. Mix thoroughly. Bash the mince by taking a handful and throwing it back into the bowl from a height 10–15 times. Use the minced meat to make meatballs. Don't make them too small. Each meatball should weigh approximately 80 g (3 oz). Toss each meatball from one hand to the other and smooth the surface with wet hands to prevent cracks. Warm each meatball in your hands and smooth it out.

5. Put the meatballs on a plate in a single layer and leave in the fridge for 30 minutes (or even overnight). This will make them even more solid.

6. Cover the tomatoes with boiling water and leave for 1 minute. Remove the skin. Put the tomatoes through a meat grinder or dice into very small cubes.

7. Fry the onions in a saucepan with oil. Add spices, herbs, and tomatoes. Simmer for 15 minutes. Season with salt. Taste to check how sweet it is. If the tomatoes are not sweet enough, add 1–2 teaspoons of sugar.

8. Take the meatballs out of the fridge and put them into the simmering sauce. Cook for 15 minutes with the lid on. Then turn them over and cook for another 15–20 minutes over low heat. Add more hot water if necessary.

9. Boil the noodles in salted water for 3–10 minutes until done. The time depends on the thickness of the noodles. Drain, add butter, and mix.

10. Plate up the noodles, put on the meatballs, and pour the sauce on top.

11. Sprinkle with finely chopped parsley.

Roasted chicken with vegetables

Ingredients

1 medium-sized chicken

2 onions

1 head of garlic

1 tbsp mustard

Salt

Ground black pepper

Ground celery

1. Rub salt, pepper and celery all over the chicken. Brush with mustard.

2. Peel the onions and the garlic.

3. Quarter the onions, crush the cloves of garlic with a knife. Put the garlic and the onions inside the chicken and tie the legs. Put the chicken into a baking tray and leave for 20 minutes.

4. Preheat the oven to 165 °C (325 °F) and roast for 2–2½ hours. Baste every 15–20 minutes with the dripping juice.

Rabbit and vegetable stew

600 g (1⅓ lb) rabbit

100 g (3½ oz) carrot

100 g (3½ oz) onion

2 potatoes

3 cloves garlic

½ tsp thyme

1 tsp dried paprika

1 tsp mustard seeds

3 tbsp oil

1. Chop the rabbit into large pieces and rub with salt.

2. Preheat the oven to 170 °C (340 °F).

3. Combine thyme, mustard seeds, paprika, and oil. Brush the meat with this mixture. Put into a baking tray, sprinkle with black pepper, cover with a lid or foil, and cook in the oven for 1 hour. Turn the pieces 3–4 times. If there is too little juice, pour in ½ glass of boiling water.

4. Peel the vegetables. Chop the carrot. Cut the potatoes into 2–4 pieces, and crush the garlic with the flat side of a knife. Put the vegetables into the baking tray next to the meat. Mix them with the juice from the meat. Cook for 20 minutes with the lid or foil on. Then uncover and cook until the potatoes get tender.

5. In general, rabbit takes about 2 hours to cook, but you need to baste the meat and the vegetables with juice every 10–15 minutes, or carefully turn the pieces.

6. When the dish is ready, sprinkle it with finely chopped parsley.

Chicken sichenyky — chicken patties

Ingredients

400 g (14 oz) chicken filet

50 g (1⅔ oz) onion

1 egg

40 g (1½ oz) white bread (approximately 3 slices)

½ glass of milk

40 g (1½ oz) butter

3–4 tbsp flour

Ground black pepper

Salt

1. Cut off the bread crust. Dice the bread and cover with milk. Leave for 20 minutes.

2. Chop the meat into very small pieces. You need to have a very sharp knife for that. It is a good idea to freeze the meat a little before cutting. If the pieces appear to be too big anyway, tenderize them with a knife.

3. Finely grate the onion. Squeeze out the juice.

4. Thoroughly squeeze the milk from the bread and mash the bread with your hands. Combine together the meat, the bread, and the onions. Season with salt and pepper. Mix well and bash the meat by taking a handful and throwing it back into the bowl.

5. Leave in the fridge for 30 minutes or longer to let all the components solidify.

6. Make small meatballs with your wet hands. Dredge in flour or breadcrumbs and fry with oil.

7. Thoroughly grease a baking tray with butter. Lay the cutlets and bake until done for 20–25 minutes. Baste with melted butter every 5 minutes.

8. If you've made your sichenyky very thin, and they've cooked through when you fried them, you don't need to bake them. Serve sichenyky with mashed potatoes.

Sichenyky are delicious juicy cutlets. Make sure you have a very sharp knife to cut the meat.

Verkhovyna chicken — chicken with porcini and sour cream

1 medium-sized chicken

40 g (1½ oz) dried porcini mushrooms

1 onion

30 g (1 oz) butter

20 g (½ oz) flour

80 g (3 oz) sour cream (not too sour)

Oil

Water or stock

Chopped parsley

Salt

1. Make the mushroom sauce. For that, rinse the mushrooms thoroughly in cold water and soak them for 1–2 hours (to speed up the process, you can cover them with boiling water). Cook until done. You'll know it when the mushrooms get tender.

2. Chop the chicken into large pieces. Leave the bones. Cut the chicken filet in half. Cut each leg into 3 pieces.

3. Fry the chicken on all sides with oil. Set aside.

4. Finely chop the cooked mushrooms and fry a little with butter until you feel the delicious smell of fried mushrooms. Add finely chopped onions. Season with salt and pepper. Fry until the onions get tender. Add the sour cream and reduce the heat. If you don't like the taste of sour cream in the dish, you can use 20% fat cream instead.

5. Combine the flour with water. Make a smooth batter without lumps. Stir into the mushrooms and sour cream mixture. Bring to a boil. Pour this sauce over the fried chicken and stew for 20–25 minutes. Add water or stock when the sauce gets too thick.

Chicken paprikash, or Chirke

Ingredients

1 medium-sized chicken

3 onions

300 g (10½ oz) bell peppers

2 tbsp ground paprika

150 g (5⅓ oz) smoked salo (or pork belly)

30 g (1 oz) butter

Water

1. You will only need chicken thighs, drumsticks, and filet for this dish. Leave the back and the wings for soup.

2. Cut each piece of filet in half. Cut off the drumsticks. Cut the thighs in half along the bone.

3. Dice the smoked salo and melt it in a saucepan. Use this fat to fry diced onions and bell peppers. Add ground paprika and chicken parts. Season with salt.

4. Stew with the lid on over low heat. Stir regularly. Add more water if the juice evaporates.

5. Fry the flour without oil until light-golden. Add the flour to the sour cream (not the other way around) and mix thoroughly to prevent any lumps. Once the meat becomes very tender and starts falling apart, add the sour cream with the flour and cook for 3 minutes.

6. At the very end, add the butter and mix everything until smooth.

Buckwheat with rabbit liver

Ingredients

250 g (9 oz) buckwheat	Oil
2 onions	Black pepper
500 g (1 lb) rabbit liver	Salt
50 g (1⅔ oz) butter	

1. Sort out the buckwheat. Wash and cover with cold water (500 ml (2 cups or 1 pt) of water per 250 g (9 oz) of buckwheat). Bring to a boil, turn down the heat, and simmer for 15 minutes with the lid on. Remove from the heat and leave for 10 minutes. Add half of the butter and season with salt.

2. Fry the rabbit liver with oil. Chop the onion in half-moon slices and add to the liver. Fry until the onion becomes tender. Pour in 100 ml (½ cup or 3½ fl oz) of water and stew over low heat for 5–7 minutes. Add the remaining butter and season with salt and pepper. Cook for several more minutes until the gravy has thickened.

3. Serve the rabbit liver with buckwheat.

4. A pickled cucumber goes well with the dish.

Hutsul beans

Ingredients

100 g (3½ oz) dried white beans	20 g (½ oz) lard
70 g (2½ oz) smoked brisket	1 clove garlic
	Salt
1 onion	Black pepper

1. Soak the beans overnight or for 5–6 hours. Rinse. Cover with water and cook until tender. Pass through a sieve or use a blender. Squeeze the garlic, season with salt and mix everything.

2. Dice the smoked brisket and the onion. Fry with lard.

3. Put the beans into a bowl. Arrange the brisket and onion mixture on top. Pour with melted lard.

4. Serve hot.

Duck legs with cranberry sauce

Ingredients

2 duck legs

½ kg (1 lb) small new potatoes

100 g (3½ oz) various dried beans

300 g (10½ oz) small young carrots

2 tbsp fresh or frozen cranberries

1. Soak the beans for 5–6 hours and cook until done for 40–60 minutes.

2. Rub the legs with salt and lay them into a baking tray. Put the meat into a cold oven and heat it to 165 °C (325 °F). Turn the legs to prevent them from getting dry.

3. Peel the potatoes and the carrots, or simply clean them with a brush if the vegetables are young and the skin is very thin. Cover the vegetables with boiling water, season with salt, and cook until done for about 5–7 minutes.

4. When the meat is almost done, turn up the heat to 190 °C (375 °F). Drain off extra fat. Not all the fat, though. Leave about 1 cm (⅓ in) of fat in the baking tray. Add the vegetables and the beans. Season with pepper. Shake the tray a little to let the fat spread evenly. Roast until the vegetables become soft in the core and crispy on the outside.

5. Take out the baking tray and add the cranberries. Mix everything.

Cranberry sauce for duck

Ingredients

1 onion

150 g (5⅓ oz) cranberries

2 tbsp duck fat

1 tsp honey

1. Finely chop the onion and fry with duck fat. Add the cranberries and stew for 7–10 minutes. Add a pinch of salt and honey. Strain the sauce through a sieve.

Crispy-skin duck with apples

Ingredients

1 duck

7 green apples

1 tbsp mustard

3 tbsp honey

Salt

Ground black pepper

1. Take half of the apples and cut each apple into 4–6 pieces. Remove the core.

2. Generously rub salt and pepper all over the duck both outside and inside. Brush with mustard and put the apples inside. Fix with toothpicks or sew up the cavity.

3. Put the duck into a deep baking pan facing the breast down. Put into the cold oven.

4. Heat the oven to 165 °C (325 °F).

5. Roast the duck for about 1½ hours. Baste with melted fat every 15–20 minutes.

6. Melt the honey over low heat.

7. Brush the duck with honey. Roast for another 30 minutes and turn the duck. If there is too much fat, drain some.

8. If the duck breast is still too hard, don't baste it with honey yet. It must be almost cooked through. Otherwise, keep on roasting and basting with fat.

9. 40 minutes before the duck is ready, start basting it with honey every 10 minutes. If the duck is too pale, turn up the heat to 175 °C (350 °F) . If it is the other way around, cover with foil.

10. 15–20 minutes before the dish is ready, cut the remaining apples into pieces and arrange them in the baking pan next to the duck. These apples will be crispier and tastier than those inside the duck. You can also put some other vegetables into the melted fat, such as half-cooked potatoes or carrots.

113

Fried brain

Ingredients

400 g (14 oz) beef brain

2 eggs

½ tsp peppercorns

1 bay leaf

1 onion

2 cloves garlic

2 tbsp apple cider vinegar

Salt

1. Cover the brain with cold water and soak for 2 hours. Change water every 30 minutes. Take off the membranes that can be easily removed.

2. Cover the brain with boiling water and leave for 1 minute. Take out and remove the remaining membranes.

3. Bring the water to the boil. Add vinegar (1 tablespoon of vinegar per 1 liter (4 cups or 2 pt) of water), garlic, peeled onion, spices, and salt. Put the brain into the boiling water and cook over low heat for 30 minutes.

4. Leave to cool. Cut into slices.

5. Whisk the eggs with salt. Heat the frying pan with oil. Dip the brain slices in the egg and fry on both sides.

Fish with vegetables

500 g (1 lb) zander fillet (or similar fish)

2 onions

1 beet

1 big carrot

2 potatoes

1 bell pepper

Salt

Oil

Ground black pepper

1. Boil the beet and the carrot. Leave to cool a little.

2. Cut the zander filet into pieces 100–150 g (3½ – 5⅓ oz) each.

3. Sprinkle with salt and put on a preheated frying pan with a generous amount of oil. Put the fish with the skin down. Don't fry the fish on the other side, but only baste it with the oil from the frying pan. Put the fish on a baking tray or distribute among several ramekins.

4. Peel the potatoes and the onions. Clean the bell pepper. Peel the cooked beet and the carrot as well. Dice all the vegetables in uniform cubes.

5. Fry the potatoes over high heat until half done. Season with salt and pepper. Put the potatoes next to the fish.

6. Pour more oil into the frying pan. Fry the onions, beet, carrot, and bell pepper. Sprinkle with salt and pepper. Put the vegetables next to the fish, either on the baking tray or in the ramekins. Cover with a lid or with foil.

7. Bake for 30–35 minutes until the potatoes are cooked through.

Zakarpattia trout with stewed tomatoes

Ingredients

1 trout

1 lemon

120 g (4 oz) cranberries

4 tomatoes

3 onions

Chopped parsley and dill

1. Scale the fish, remove the entrails, gills and fins. Wash.

2. Rub the fish with salt and black pepper. Put several slices of lemon inside. Stuff with chopped greens and cranberries, putting in as much as you can.

3. Preheat the oven to 190 °C (375 °F).

4. Cut one onion into thick rings. Lay them on a baking tray. Put the trout on top. In this way, you will make sure that the lower part of the fish will also get roasted rather than stewed in the juice.

5. Cover the fish with foil and cook in the oven for 25–30 minutes.

6. Cut the remaining onions and tomatoes in half moon slices. Melt the butter. Fry the onions with the butter over medium heat until translucent. Add the tomatoes and the remaining cranberries. Crush some cranberries with a fork right in the frying pan. Leave the other cranberries as they are. Season with salt, black pepper, and sugar. Simmer for 3–4 minutes until all extra liquid evaporates.

7. Take the fish out of the oven. Remove the greens and the lemon. Remove the skin and separate the meat from the bones. Drizzle with lemon juice and serve with stewed tomatoes.

Zander tovchenyky – fish patties

Ingredients

600 g (1⅓ lb) zander

2 eggs

4 slices of stale white bread

½ tsp salt

½ tsp peppercorns

Ground nutmeg

½ tsp allspice

½ onion

1. Clean the fish. Remove the skin and the bones. Cut the fish into small pieces and mash them in a mortar. If you don't have a mortar, you can gather all the pieces together, cover with cling wrap and mash with a tenderizer or a baking roll.

2. Cut off the bread crust. Soak the slices of bread in cold milk for 15 minutes. Squeeze out the extra liquid.

3. Finely grate the onion and squeeze out the extra juice. Grind allspice and peppercorns in the mortar.

4. Separate the egg whites from the yolks. Whip the egg whites into foam (as if for meringue). The foam must be very stiff so that it will remain inside the bowl if you turn it upside down.

5. Mix the yolks together with the spices, onion, bread, and zander. Mix thoroughly. Slightly bash the mince by taking a handful and throwing it back into the bowl 5–6 times.

6. Add the egg whites and mix carefully.

7. Heat the frying pan with a generous amount of oil to make sure that tovchenyky will fry well on the edges as well.

8. Take a little tovchenyky in your oiled-up hands (this will prevent the mince from sticking to your hands) or simply use a spoon to put the tovchenyky into the frying pan.

9. Fry on both sides with well-heated oil over medium heat. Serve with mashed potatoes.

Carp with mamalyha

Ingredients

50 g (1⅔ oz) cornmeal

200 ml (1 cup or 7 fl oz) water

1 piece of carp

Salt

1 pinch caraway

100 g (3½ oz) brynza (or any other soft fresh cheese, e.g. ricotta)

½ tbsp butter

1. Sift the cornmeal.

2. Bring the water to a boil. Stir in the cornmeal and cook for 15 minutes over medium heat, stirring constantly.

3. Stir mamalyha thoroughly with a wooden spoon and cover with a lid. Cook over low heat for 10 minutes until almost all the liquid evaporates and the porridge starts pulling away from the sides of the pot.

4. Rub the fish with salt and ground caraway. Fry over medium heat on both sides. Remove from heat and take off the skin.

5. Plate up mamalyha. Put a piece of butter and some mashed brynza on top.

Scrambled eggs on toast with spinach

Ingredients

4 eggs	2 slices of bread
1 tomato	25 g (1 oz) butter
1 bunch spinach	Dill

1. Cover the tomato with boiling water, leave for 1 minute, and take off the skin. Remove the seeds and slice thinly.

2. Thoroughly wash the spinach and dry. Sort out the dill and choose the thinnest stalks. Combine with the sliced tomatoes and spinach. You can also add some fresh mint leaves.

3. Make toasts without oil.

4. Whisk the eggs with salt. Melt the butter on a frying pan, turn down the heat and pour in the egg mixture. Let the eggs cook a little and then stir. Repeat until the eggs are cooked through. Don't overcook the eggs, though. They shouldn't be too dry.

5. Spread some butter on toast. Arrange some spinach and tomato mixture, and then put some scrambled eggs on top.

Zakarpattia fried eggs with salo

Ingredients

2 eggs	½ onion
50 g (1⅔ oz) smoked salo, pork belly or brisket	Black pepper
	Salt

1. Thinly slice the salo and fry over low heat.

2. Add the chopped onion and cook until translucent.

3. Add the eggs, cover with a lid for 2 minutes. Take the lid off and cook until the eggs reach a desired condition.

4. Season with salt and pepper.

Fried eggs with brynza and veggies

Ingredients

70 g (2½ oz) brynza (or any other soft fresh cheese, e.g. ricotta)

2 tomatoes

1 bell pepper

1 onion

2 eggs

1 tbsp oil

1 tsp ground paprika

Chopped dill

Green onions

Black pepper

1. Quarter the bell pepper, remove the stem, and roast at 220 °C (425 °F) on the top wire rack until the skin gets charred. Put the pepper pieces into a plastic bag, tie and leave for 20 minutes. Remove the skin and dice into cubes.

2. Take a frying pan that you can also use in the oven. Finely chop the onion, fry with oil until tender, and leave in the frying pan.

3. Dunk the tomatoes into boiling water for 1 minute. Take out and remove the skin. Remove the seeds and dice.

4. Mash the brynza with your hands.

5. Put the brynza, tomatoes and pepper into the frying pan on top of the onions. Sprinkle with paprika. Bake in the oven at 200 °C (390 °F) for 15 minutes. Take out of the oven, stir in 2 eggs, and bake for another 15 minutes until done.

6. Season with pepper and sprinkle with finely chopped dill and green onion. Usually you don't have to add any salt since brynza is salty enough.

Steamed varenyky with potatoes and mushrooms

Ingredients

For dough:

500 g (1 lb) flour

250 g (9 oz) kefir 1% fat (or liquid drinkable yogurt), room temperature

½ tsp baking soda

½ tsp salt

For the filling:

250 g (9 oz) potatoes

1 medium-sized onion

70 g (2½ oz) mushrooms

For the cracklings:

100 g (3½ oz) pork belly (choose a piece with more meat and less fat)

1 medium-sized onion

1. Peel the potatoes and cut into 4 pieces. Cover with boiling water, add salt, and cook until done. Make sure you don't overcook the potatoes. Drain the water and cook a little over low heat to let all the remaining liquid evaporate. Mash the potatoes without adding any water or milk. You don't have to make it very smooth. It's okay to leave some little lumps. Leave to cool with the lid on so that the potatoes don't get dark.

2. Finely chop the mushrooms and the onion. Fry with oil. Drain extra oil and combine the mushroom and onion mixture with the potatoes. Season with salt and pepper to taste. Put aside with the lid on.

3. Mix together the baking soda, salt, and kefir. Leave for 20 minutes until bubbles appear on the surface. Add the flour in small portions. You might need less flour eventually, depending on the thickness of the kefir. Knead the dough. It must be soft and elastic. Cover with a lid or wrap it in cling wrap. Leave for 20 minutes.

4. Divide the dough into uniform pieces. Varenyky must be big. Knead each piece of dough a little. While doing so, cover the other pieces with a towel or cling wrap so that they don't get dry. Roll out each piece of dough into a circle approximately 5–7 mm thick. Put 1 teaspoon of filling in the middle. It will be more convenient if you roll some filling into a ball first. Wet the edges of the circle and carefully pinch them to seal.

5. Take a large pot and fill ⅔ of it with water. Pull a piece of cheesecloth over the pot and tie it with a string. Make sure it is secure. Bring the water to a boil. Carefully put varenyky on the cheesecloth and cover with a lid or a large bowl. Cook for 7–8 minutes.

6. In the meantime, cut the pork belly and the onion. Fry over medium heat until golden brown. Sprinkle this mixture over the varenyky once they are cooked. Toss to prevent them from sticking.

Varenyky–khvalenyky with spinach and cheese — praiseworthy varenyky

Ingredients

220 g (½ lb) flour

2 egg yolks

60 ml (¼ cup) cold water

160 g (5⅔ oz) spinach

250 g (9 oz) brynza (or any other soft fresh cheese, e.g. ricotta)

60 g (2 oz) butter

Salt

1. Sift the flour into a bowl. Make a "well" in the piled-up flour, add the yolks, salt, and half of the water. Start mixing the ingredients, adding more water in small portions. You might need less water eventually, depending on the flour. Knead the dough for 7–10 minutes until it becomes elastic. Roll out the dough into a ball and wrap in cling wrap or put it into some container and cover with a lid. Leave in the fridge for 30 minutes.

2. Sort out the spinach, wash thoroughly, and cover with boiling water. Leave for 1 minute, drain, squeeze out all the liquid, and cut coarsely.

3. Knead the brynza with your hands or put through a meat grinder if it is hard. Combine with the spinach and leave for 10 minutes.

4. Take the dough out of the fridge and divide it roughly into 4 pieces to make it easier to roll out.

5. Roll out each piece very thinly. Cut out circles of around 8 cm (3 in) in diameter.

6. Take the filling and drain the juice if there is any. Roll the filling into small balls and put them in the middle of the circles. Wet the edges and pinch to seal.

7. Take out varenyky with a skimmer and put them in a bowl with butter. Sprinkle with chopped green onions.

Here's something very important! Cook varenyky in boiling water for 1½ minutes. If you cook them longer than 2 minutes, the dough and the cheese will become loose.

Classic varenyky with liver

For dough:

120 ml (½ cup, 4 fl oz) water

200 g (7 oz) all-purpose flour

20 g (1 tbsp) butter

2 pinches of salt

For filling:

250 g (9 oz) veal liver (chicken liver will also do, but don't use pork liver as it tastes bitter)

3 onions

2 tbsp butter

1 tbsp oil

Salt

1. Mix the flour and salt in a large bowl. Bring the water to a boil along with the butter. Then pour this into the flour in a thin stream and stir with a spoon. Hand knead for 3-5 minutes. Start gently, as the dough will be hot at first. Wrap the dough in plastic wrap and leave on the table for 30 minutes.

2. Cut the liver into large pieces, plunge in boiling water, and cook for 7–10 minutes. Take out the liver and leave to cool a little. Remove all the membranes and veins. Put through a meat grinder.

3. Finely chop the onion and fry with butter. Add 1 tablespoon of oil to prevent sticking. Remove half of the onions. Add the ground liver into the frying pan and continue frying for another 3–4 minutes. Leave to cool a little.

4. Divide the dough into 2–3 pieces to make it easier to roll. Roll out the dough into a very thin sheet and cut out circles of around 8 cm (3 in) in diameter. You can use a glass or a special cutter.

5. Put 1 rounded teaspoon of filling on each circle. Wet the edge and pinch to seal.

6. Cook in boiling water for 1½ minutes. The dough is very thin and the filling is already cooked through.

7. Sprinkle with the fried onions that you have put aside. Add a little more butter.

Kulish with giblets — millet porridge with giblets

Ingredients

150 g (5⅓ oz) millet

500 ml (2 cups or 1 pt) water

1 onion

70 g (2½ oz) carrot

50 g (1⅔ oz) salo

400 g (14 oz) chicken liver and hearts

1 tbsp oil

1. Sort out the chicken hearts, cut off the tops, and cut in half.

2. Thoroughly wash the millet. Cover with water and bring to a boil. Reduce the heat. Add the hearts.

3. The millet will be done in about 20–25 minutes. Add more water if necessary.

4. Dice the salo into small cubes, put on a frying pan, and melt over low heat.

5. Use this melted fat to fry the chopped onion and the grated carrot. Add to the millet together with the cracklings. Leave the melted fat in the frying pan.

6. Cut the liver and remove the membranes. Pour 1 tablespoon of oil into the frying pan and fry the liver.

7. When the millet is almost done, add the liver. Season with salt and mix. Boil for another 2 minutes. Remove from the heat and leave for 15 minutes.

Rice stewed with porcini mushrooms

Ingredients

100 g (3½ oz) long-grain rice

100 g (3½ oz) porcini mushrooms (frozen mushrooms will do, but don't take dried ones)

1 onion

1 clove garlic

30 g (1 oz) butter

1 tbsp oil

1. Wash the rice thoroughly, changing the water several times. Soak for 30 minutes. Drain.

2. Thoroughly clean all sand from the mushrooms and cut them into pieces.

3. Dice the onion into small cubes, crush the garlic with a knife, and chop very finely.

4. Melt ⅔ of the butter on a frying pan. Add oil and fry the onions until translucent over very low heat. Add the mushrooms and fry for several minutes until golden-brown. Add the garlic and rice. Cook for 1 more minute. Season with salt.

5. Pour in ½ glass of water. Cook until the rice is done without covering the frying pan. Constantly add more water in small portions and stir from time to time.

6. When the rice is done, all the water must have evaporated. Add the remaining butter and mix. Cover with a lid and leave for 5 minutes.

7. Season with black pepper and sprinkle with chopped parsley.

Baked new potatoes

Ingredients

1 kg (2 lb) new potatoes

60 g (2 oz) butter

2 tbsp oil

Salt

Chopped dill

Green onions

Sour cream

1. Cover the potatoes with cold water and soak for 15–20 minutes. Scrape with a knife. Preheat the oven to 200 °C (390 °F).

2. Drain the potatoes and dry them a little over heat. Add oil and diced butter. Toss the pot to grease the potatoes evenly. Season with salt.

3. Lay the potatoes on a baking tray in a single layer. Bake until nicely brown and crispy. Serve with sour cream and chopped greens.

Baked potatoes with salo and red onion

Ingredients

600 g (1⅓ lb) potatoes

100 g (3½ oz) salted salo (or pork belly) with meat layers

2 red onions

2 tbsp oil

1 head garlic

Salt

Ground black pepper

Green onion

1. Peel the potatoes and cut into 4–6 pieces. Cover with boiling water, add salt, and boil until half-cooked for about 10–15 minutes. The potatoes should remain hard inside.

2. Heat the oven to 200 °C (390 °F).

3. Drain the potatoes, dry a little over low heat, add oil, and mix, tossing the potatoes in the pot. Add a little more salt.

4. Cut the onions into 6 pieces. Cut the head of garlic in half.

5. Lay the potatoes, onions, and garlic in a single layer on a baking tray. Put slices of salo on top. Bake until golden and crisp. When the garlic starts to burn, just remove it and put aside. It has given away all its flavor.

6. Sprinkle with chopped green onions and black pepper before serving.

Here's the best way to cook potatoes! A crunchy crust comes with a delicious soft core.

Tsybulnyky — onion fritters with pureéd carrots

The dish tastes especially delicious when served with stewed carrots. Sometimes tsybulnyky ("tsybulia" is Ukrainian for "onion") are served with sour cream, but the taste is completely different. The batter should be runny and flow freely over the frying pan to make sure that the onion fritters are really thin. So, if the eggs are small, add three instead of two.

Ingredients

4 onions

2 eggs

1 tbsp flour

½ tsp baking soda

1 tsp vinegar

2 carrots

1 tsp tomato paste

Oil

Salt

Ground black pepper

1. Chop 3 onions very finely. Slightly squeeze with your hands to make them softer.

2. Add the eggs, flour, salt, pepper, and baking soda mixed with vinegar. Mix everything.

3. Heat a frying pan with oil, spoon the onion batter, and fry over medium heat. Flatten the fritters with a spoon so that the onions lie in a single layer and fry well.

4. Cut the remaining onion in half-moon slices and fry with oil. Grate the carrots using large holes, add to the onions, and fry, stirring regularly to prevent sticking. Add the tomato paste, ½ glass of water, and salt. Stew until tender to let all the water evaporate. If the carrots are not very sweet, add 1 teaspoon of sugar.

The main thing is to chop the onions as finely as possible and cook over medium heat so that they fry really well.

Fried potatoes with mushrooms

Ingredients

400 g (14 oz) potatoes

200 g (7 oz) portobello mushrooms (or any other mushrooms)

1 onion

1 clove garlic

Oil

½ tsp peppercorns

1 bay leaf

1. Peel the potatoes and cut into 8–10 pieces. Cut the mushrooms into 2–4 pieces.

2. Coarsely chop the onion and fry until translucent. Add the mushrooms and cook until golden-brown. Put aside.

3. Pour more oil into the frying pan. Heat well. Pat dry the potatoes and start frying. Stir very seldomly. Don't stir until the crust forms. Season with black pepper and bay leaf.

4. Keep frying the potatoes. Add the mushrooms and salt. Cook everything together until golden-brown.

5. Turn down the heat and cover with a lid. Cook until the potatoes are fork-tender.

6. Serve with pickled cucumbers and tomatoes.

Kremzlyky – potato fritters with cracklings

Ingredients

1 onion

4 medium-sized high-starch potatoes

1 egg

150 g (5⅓ oz) smoked salo (or pork belly)

Green onions

Ground black pepper

Sour cream

1. Use medium-sized holes on your grater to shred the onion and the peeled potatoes. Mix immediately. It's important to grate the onion first as it prevents the potatoes from getting dark.

2. Season with salt, stir in the egg, and mix thoroughly.

3. Spoon the mixture on a preheated frying pan with oil. Flatten a little so that the fritter is thin in the middle and cooks well.

4. Fry over medium heat on both sides.

5. Dice the smoked salo into small cubes. Fry over medium heat until golden brown.

6. Serve kremzlyky with cracklings, chopped green onions, black pepper, and sour cream.

Potato halushky with fried chicken

Ingredients

200 g (7 oz) chicken filet

2 onions

500 g (1 lb) potatoes

1 egg yolk

4 tbsp flour

1 tbsp oil

2 tbsp butter

1. Boil the potatoes in jackets. Don't overcook. Peel and grate finely. Cover with a lid so that the potatoes don't get dark.

2. Leave to cool a little with the lid on. Add the yolk and the flour. Make sure the potatoes are not too hot. Otherwise the yolk will get cooked.

3. Knead the dough for 4–5 minutes. Make a roll of approximately 3 cm (1 in) in diameter. Cut into pieces 2–2½ cm (¾ – 1 in) long. Slightly flatten each piece with your finger or with a knife for a nicer look.

4. Cook in salted boiling water for 40 seconds. Don't cook halushky longer than 1 minute as they are almost done already. Take out of water with a skimmer and put on a plate.

5. Cut the chicken into long thin slices. Cut the onion in half-moon slices. Combine 1 tablespoon of butter with 1 tablespoon of oil and fry the chicken together with the onion over high heat until golden-brown. Season with salt. Add the halushky into the frying pan and heat everything together. Stir very carefully because halushky are very delicate.

6. Sprinkle with chopped greens and black pepper.

Kartoplianyky with meat — stuffed potato patties

Ingredients

600 g (1⅓ lb) potatoes

1 egg

2 tbsp flour + flour for dredging

1 onion

400 g (14 oz) beef

1. Plunge the meat into boiling water and cook until done. Take out of the water, leave to cool a little, and put through a meat grinder.

2. Dice the onion and fry with oil. Add the minced meat and 2–3 tablespoons of stock. Cook until the onion gets tender. Add some more stock — just enough to let the filling remain juicy. Season with salt and pepper to taste.

3. Peel the potatoes, cut into 4 pieces, and cook in salted water until done. Make sure you don't overcook the potatoes. Drain the potatoes and dry them thoroughly over low heat to let all the liquid evaporate. Mash the potatoes and cover with a lid to prevent them from getting dark. Leave to cool.

4. Add the egg and the flour to the mashed potatoes. Mix everything. The mixture should be smooth and without any lumps.

5. Take a spoonful of potatoes and roll into a ball. Flatten and put a spoonful of meat filling in the middle. Pinch to seal and give it a nice shape.

6. Dredge kartoplianyky in flour and fry over medium heat on both sides.

7. Serve with sour cream.

Baked kartoplianyky with mushrooms — baked stuffed potato patties

600 g (1⅓ lb) potatoes

1 egg

2 tbsp flour + flour for dredging

1 onion

200 g (7 oz) portobello mushrooms

1 egg yolk

Salt

1. Dice the mushrooms and the onion. First, fry the onions until translucent, then add the mushrooms and cook over low heat until the onion becomes tender. Season with salt and pepper to taste.

2. Peel the potatoes, cut into 4 pieces, and cook in salted water until done. Make sure you don't overcook the potatoes. Drain the potatoes and dry them thoroughly over low heat to let all the liquid evaporate. Mash the potatoes and cover with a lid to prevent them from getting dark. Leave to cool.

3. Add the egg and the flour to the mashed potatoes. Mix everything. The mixture should be smooth and without any lumps.

4. Take a spoonful of potato mixture and roll into a ball. Flatten and put a spoonful of mushrooms in the middle. Pinch to seal and give it a nice round shape. Dredge in flour.

5. Whisk the egg yolk with 1 teaspoonful of water. Brush kartoplianyky with this mixture and lay on a greased baking tray.

6. Bake in the oven at 200 °C (390 °F) until they are a beautiful golden color.

Dranyky — potato fritters with mushrooms

To make sure your dranyky are tasty and solid, use potatoes with a high starch content. Never soak potatoes after peeling. Just rinse them quickly. To check how starchy your potatoes are, cut a potato in half and join the two pieces together. If they stick to each other, it means that the potato is high in starch. If not, add 1–2 teaspoons of starch per 4 medium-sized potatoes.

Ingredients

4 medium-sized high-starch potatoes

1 onion

1 egg

150 g (5⅓ oz) porcini mushrooms

6–7 tbsp fat sour cream (not very sour)

2 cloves garlic

Oil

30 g (1 oz) butter

Chopped parsley

Salt

1. Use the smallest holes on your grater to shred the onion and the peeled potatoes. Mix together. Onions will prevent the potatoes from getting dark. If there is too much juice, drain a little. Do not squeeze.

2. Season with salt. Stir in the egg and mix. Spoon the mixture onto a preheated frying pan with oil. Flatten a little so that the fritter is thin in the middle and cooks well.

3. Fry over medium heat on both sides.

4. Make the sauce. Clean sand from the porcini mushrooms and slice.

5. Melt the butter and fry the mushrooms. At the very end add the chopped garlic, reduce the heat, and cook for another 2 minutes.

6. Add the sour cream (you can use 25% fat cream instead) and simmer over low heat until the smell of the sour cream goes away. Season with salt.

7. Sprinkle with chopped parsley and serve hot.

Tertiukhy — potato fritters in Hutsul style

Ingredients

3 onions

6 high-starch potatoes

1 egg

2 level tsp starch

400 g (14 oz) pork neck

4–5 tbsp fat sour cream (not very sour)

1 tbsp butter

Ground black pepper

Oil

Salt

1. Finely grate 2 onions and half of the peeled potatoes. Grate the remaining onions using large holes. Mix everything immediately to prevent the potatoes from getting dark. Squeeze out extra juice.

2. Add salt, egg and starch. Mix everything and shape round balls 1–1½ cm (⅓ – ½ in) high.

3. Preheat the oven to 200 °C (390 °F).

4. Preheat a frying pan. Fry the tertiukhy with a large amount of oil so that the edges fry as well.

5. Lay the fritters on a baking tray and bake in the oven for about 30 minutes. Baste with butter to prevent them from drying.

6. In the meantime cook the meat. Chop the pork into small pieces. Grate the onion. Preheat the frying pan and fry the meat with oil. Add the onions and stew until the meat is fork-tender. Add water in small portions from time to time. Season with salt and pepper.

7. When the meat is cooked through, pour in the sour cream and stew for 5–7 minutes over low heat until the smell of the sour cream goes away.

8. Remove the tertiukhy from the oven. Put a spoonful of meat on each fritter. Garnish with dill.

Potatoes baked on salt with sour cream sauce and cracklings

Ingredients

4 big potatoes

150 g (5⅓ oz) pork belly

1 cucumber

300 g (10½ oz) sour cream 25% fat

Ground black pepper

½ kg (1 lb) coarse grain salt

Dill

1. Preheat the oven to 180 °C (350 °F).

2. Thoroughly wash the potatoes and clean them with a brush. Don't peel. Dry the potatoes. Take 4 slices of pork belly. Cut each potato in half lengthwise, but not fully. Wedge a slice of pork belly between the potato halves.

3. Spread the salt over the baking tray. Put the potatoes with the cut facing down. Bake until done for 1½ – 2 hours.

4. In the meantime make the sauce. Dice the cucumber into very small cubes and mix with the sour cream. Finely chop the remaining pork belly and fry in its own fat until the fat melts and the cracklings get crunchy.

5. Take out the potatoes and shake off the salt. Cut fully in half. Serve with the sauce and the cracklings.

6. Sprinkle with black pepper and dill if you like.

Corn halushky with brynza

Ingredients

50 g (1⅔ oz) corn grits

250 ml (1 cup or 9 fl oz) water

1 medium-sized potato

200 g (7 oz) brynza

1 level tbsp flour

Flour for dusting

1. Cover the corn grits with water and cook over low heat for 20–25 minutes until done, stirring regularly. If you have finely ground corn grits, use less water or cook over higher heat until the water evaporates. The corn porridge must be very thick.

2. Boil the potato in a jacket, peel and grate finely. Combine with the porridge, add 1 tablespoon of flour, sprinkle with salt, and make the dough.

3. Dust the table with flour, put the dough on the table and knead for 3–4 minutes.

4. Dust with flour again and make a roll of about 5 cm (2 in) in diameter.

5. Cut the roll into pieces 3–3½ cm (1–1⅓ in) long. Roll a bit to round the edges.

6. Take a deep frying pan and heat it with a large amount of oil (about 4 cm or 1½ in) and deep-fry the halushky until golden-brown.

7. Be careful! Don't overcook the halushky. Otherwise they may crack.

8. Put the halushky on a paper towel to absorb extra grease. Plate up and sprinkle with fork-mashed brynza (or any other soft fresh cheese, e.g. ricotta) while they are still hot.

Pastry and bread

Rye bread

Ingredients

250 g (9 oz) wheat flour

150 g (5⅓ oz) rye flour

15 g (½ oz) fresh yeast

1 tsp sugar

250 ml (1 cup or 9 fl oz) warm water

2 tsp salt

1 tsp butter

4 tbsp pumpkin seeds

1. Dissolve the yeast in warm water (35–40 °C / 95–105 °F). Add sugar and half of the wheat and rye flour. Mix thoroughly, cover with a towel, and leave for 30–60 minutes until the mixture doubles in size.

2. Add salt and the remaining flour. Make the dough. Add more wheat flour if necessary. Then add 1 teaspoonful of soft butter and half of the pumpkin seeds. Knead the dough for 5 minutes.

3. Make a round loaf, put it into a baking tray lined with baking paper, make decorative slashes with a sharp knife, cover with a towel, and let it proof for 1 hour. The loaf must double in size. From now on do not touch the dough.

4. Preheat the oven to 210 °C (410 °F). Put a bowl with boiling hot water at the bottom of the oven that will give away steam while baking.

5. Carefully brush the loaf with salted water and sprinkle with seeds. Do not touch the bread with your hands.

6. Bake in the oven for 40–50 minutes.

7. Remove the bowl with water after 25 minutes of baking.

8. Take out the bread. Let it cool a little. When it is done, the loaf will sound hollow if you tap on it.

Classic bread

1. Dissolve the yeast and the sugar in half of the warm water. The water should be lukewarm rather than hot because any temperature above 45 °C (115 °F) kills yeast.

2. Sift the flour into a bowl and mix it with salt. Make a well in the middle and pour in the water and yeast mixture. Mix, moving from the edges to the center.

3. Pour in the remaining hot water and make the dough. Add water slowly. You might need less water eventually. However, if you think you need more water, add some.

4. Knead the dough for at least 5–7 minutes. If the dough is too wet and sticks to your hands, dust it with flour.

5. Roll the dough into a ball and make a deep slash on the top with a sharp knife. Put the dough into a deep bowl and wrap with a towel in several layers. Let the dough proof for 40–60 minutes until it doubles in size. For that, you need a warm draft-free place. If the weather is very hot, the dough will rise wherever you leave it. Otherwise, put it near the radiator, electric heater, or into the oven that you've preheated to 40 °C (105 °F), not more. Open the oven every 15 minutes for 1 minute.

6. Your dough may take more time to rise. It's okay. The key point is to let it double in size. When it happens, knead the dough for another 2 minutes.

7. Now shape the loaf. For that, roll the dough into a ball. To get rid of the cracks, take the dough with its smooth side facing up and pull all the cracks downwards as if you are hiding them underneath.

8. Grease a baking tray or line it with baking paper. Put the dough inside and make 2–3 decorative cuts, cover with a towel, and let it rise one more time in a warm place. This will take about 30–40 minutes. Don't touch the dough.

9. Preheat the oven to 210 °C (410 °F).

10. Dissolve a pinch of salt and baking soda in 1 teaspoon of water. Carefully brush the loaf with this mixture and dust with a little flour.

11. Carefully put into the oven and bake for 30–40 minutes. When it is done, the loaf will sound hollow if you tap on it.

12. If you bake the bread in a baking mold, take it out immediately and put it on a wire rack. Otherwise the bottom may get overcooked. Leave the bread to cool.

Bread with onion and greens

Ingredients

For the bread:

15 g (½ oz) fresh yeast

1 tbsp sugar

1 level tbsp salt

280 ml (1¼ cup or 9½ fl oz) water

500 g (1 lb) flour

For the filling:

1 tbsp butter

½ bunch dill

1 red onion

1 tsp sugar

½ tsp salt

1. Make the dough in the same way as in the Classic bread recipe above.

2. Cut the onion in half-moon slices. Fry with butter until tender. Add salt and sugar. Leave to cool.

3. Finely chop the dill.

4. After the dough has risen, roll it out into a sheet. Put the onions evenly over the entire sheet and sprinkle with dill.

5. Tuck the edges and roll up into a log.

6. Grease the baking tray or line it with baking paper. Put the loaf on the baking tray, make several cuts with a sharp knife, and dust with flour. Cover with a towel and leave in a warm place. From now on do not touch the dough!

7. Preheat the oven to 200 °C (390 °F).

8. When the dough doubles in size, carefully put it into the oven for 30 minutes.

9. Check if the bread is ready. When it is done, the loaf will sound hollow if you tap on it.

Pampushky — Ukrainian garlic bread

Ingredients

300 g (10½ oz) flour	½ tsp salt
100 ml (½ cup or 3½ fl oz) water	1 tbsp oil
8 g (⅓ oz) fresh yeast or 3 g (1 tsp) dry yeast	1 egg
1 tbsp water	

1. Dissolve the yeast in warm water. The water should be lukewarm rather than hot because any temperature above 45 °C (115 °F) kills yeast. Add ¼ of the flour and mix thoroughly. Cover with a towel and leave in a warm place.

2. If the weather is very hot, the dough will rise wherever you put it. Otherwise, put it near the radiator, electric heater, or into the oven that you've preheated to 40 °C (104 °F), not more. Open the oven every 15 minutes for 1 minute.

3. Dissolve sugar and salt in 1½ tablespoons of water. When the dough doubles or triples in size, add the sugar and salt solution, the remaining flour, and oil. Knead the dough for 3–5 minutes. Add more flour if necessary, but make sure the dough is not too tough.

4. Cover with a towel and leave the dough to proof for 1½ hours in a warm place. The dough must expand several times its size.

5. Dust the table with flour. Put the dough on the table and divide into small round buns (about 30 g (1 oz) each). Shape pampushky with a smooth top. To avoid cracks, stretch the dough and pull the uneven parts downward as if you're hiding them underneath.

6. Grease the baking tray or line it with baking paper. Put pampushky on the tray side by side at about ½ cm from one another. Cover with a towel and leave for 30–40 minutes to let them proof.

7. Preheat the oven to 180 °C (350 °F). Whisk 1 egg yolk with 1 teaspoon of water. Carefully brush the pampushky with this mixture and bake in the oven for 20–25 minutes.

Garlic oil for pampushky

Ingredients

4 cloves garlic	½ bunch dill
3 tsp water	½ tsp salt
3 tsp oil	

1. Crush the dill with garlic and salt in a mortar. Add oil and water. Mix thoroughly. Serve together with pampushky.

Hutsul palianytsia

Ingredients

550 g (1¼ lb) wheat flour

200 g (7 oz) cornmeal

380 ml (1⅔ cups or 13 fl oz) water

90 g (3 oz) kefir (or liquid drinkable yogurt)

20 g (½ oz) fresh yeast

½ tbsp sugar

15 g (1 tbsp) butter

1 tsp salt

1. Dissolve the yeast in warm water (30–35 °C / 85–95 °F), add half of the wheat flour and mix thoroughly to avoid any lumps. Cover with a towel and leave in a warm place for 1½ –2 hours to prove.

2. If the weather is very hot, the dough will rise wherever you put it. Otherwise, put it near the radiator, electric heater, or into the oven that you've preheated to 40 °C (100 °F), not more. Open the oven every 15 minutes for 1 minute.

3. The yeast mixture must expand 1½ –2 times.

4. Dissolve sugar and salt in 1 tablespoon of water. Add kefir and pour into the yeast mixture. Add the cornmeal, mix, and add the remaining wheat flour. Knead for 3–4 minutes and pour in the melted butter. Keep kneading until the dough becomes smooth and comes away from your hands easily.

5. Cover with a towel and leave in a warm place to proof for 1½ –2 hours until the dough doubles in size.

6. Shape palianytsia — a round loaf with a semi-circular slash on top. Grease the baking tray or line it with baking paper. Put palianytsia inside and let it proof in a warm place for another 20 minutes.

7. Preheat the oven to 200 °C (390 °F). Whisk 1 egg yolk with 1 teaspoon of water. Carefully brush the palianytsia with this mixture. Bake for 40–45 minutes. When it is done, the loaf will sound hollow if you tap on it.

Potato and onion pie

Ingredients

For the pie:

120 g (4 oz) butter

170 g (6 oz) flour

70 g (2½ oz) sour cream

1 tsp mustard

Salt

Black pepper

For the filling:

3–4 potatoes

4 onions

40 ml (3 tbsp) fat cream

1 egg

1. Dice the butter. Add the flour and salt. Use your fingertips to rub the flour and butter together until it resembles breadcrumbs. You can use a food processor.

2. Add the sour cream, mix everything, and roll into a ball. Wrap in cling wrap and keep in the fridge for 40 minutes.

3. Peel the potatoes and boil in salted water until done. Cut into rounds.

4. Chop the onions and fry with butter until golden brown.

5. Put the dough into the baking mold and make the edges with your wet hands. Brush with mustard. Place the potatoes first and sprinkle with salt. Then lay the onions and pour in the cream whisked with salt, pepper, and egg.

6. Bake at 170 °C (340 °F) for 40–45 minutes.

Chicken pie with slippery jack mushrooms

Ingredients

For the pie:

120 g (4 oz) butter

30 g (1 oz) powdered sugar

220 g (½ lb) flour

2 tbsp milk

1 pinch salt

For the filling:

1 red onion

100 g (3½ oz) fresh or frozen slippery jacks

100 g (3½ oz) chicken filet

25 g (1 oz) butter

2 tbsp cream

Salt

Ground black pepper

1. Bring the butter to room temperature, cut into pieces, and stir with salt and powdered sugar. Add the flour and the egg yolks. Mix everything so that the mixture resembles breadcrumbs. Pour in the milk and mix the dough very quickly before the butter starts to melt.

2. Wrap the dough in cling wrap or cover with a lid and put into the fridge for 1 hour.

3. Make the filling. Boil the chicken filet until done. Cut the onion, chicken and mushrooms into pieces.

4. Melt the butter and use it to fry the onions. Add the mushrooms and fry for another 5 minutes. Then add the chicken and season with salt and pepper. 2 minutes later pour in the cream. Simmer until all extra liquid evaporates. Leave to cool.

5. Carefully cut the dough into several pieces and roll them out a little. Make a pie crust by spreading the dough all over the baking mold and making the edges with the dough. Press and seal the seams with wet fingertips. Use the remaining dough to make strips.

6. Put the filling on the dough, make a lattice top and trim the edges.

7. Bake for 40–50 minutes at 180 °C (350 °F) on a wire rack which is a bit lower than in the middle.

8. If the bottom of your pie is too thick, the dough may end up undercooked. To avoid this, you can first blind bake the pie crust and after that add the filling. For that, spread the dough over the baking mold without the edges, line with baking paper and fill it with dried beans. Bake at 180 °C (350 °F) for 15 minutes.

Granny's pie

It is a soft and delicious pie with a fantastic smell. Besides, it is very easy to make. Any kind of jam will do as a filling for this pie — apricots, plums, whatever. However, it shouldn't have too much juice. Try to remove any extra liquid from the fruit. Don't put too much flour into the dough. It must remain very soft and even stick to your hands. If it happens, wet your hands and keep on working with the dough, but don't add any more flour.

Ingredients

For the pie:

100 ml (½ cup or 3½ fl oz) milk

13 g (½ oz) fresh yeast

3 egg yolks

80 g (3 oz) butter

100 g (3½ oz) sugar

1 pinch salt

Flour

For the filling:

2–3 apples

2 tbsp sugar

2 tbsp water

⅓ tsp cinnamon

1. Dissolve the yeast in 2 tablespoons of warm water (30–35 °C / 85–95 °F). Leave in a warm place for 20 minutes.

2. Warm up the milk and add diced butter. Melt the butter.

3. Whisk the egg yolks with the sugar, add butter and milk mixture (room temperature), yeast, salt, and flour. Add the flour slowly so that the dough does not end up too tight. The dough must be stretchy and wet. Thoroughly mix all the components and knead. Cover with a towel or cling wrap and leave in a warm place to proof. You can also use the oven (preheated to 40 °C / 105 °F), a radiator or electric heater. Leave for 1–1½ hours. The time depends on the temperature in the room.

4. Make the filling. First make the syrup with 2 tablespoons of sugar and 2 tablespoons of water. Add the peeled and sliced apples. Cook over high heat so that the juice evaporates quickly while the apples don't get too soggy. Add the cinnamon. Remove from the heat and chill.

5. Preheat the oven to 180 °C (350 °F). Grease the baking mold with butter.

6. When the dough rises, take ⅔ of the dough, spread it over the baking mold, and make the edges. Use the remaining dough to make thin rolls by stretching them with wet hands. Try to make them uniform.

7. Put the apple filling on the dough and make a lattice top. Seal with wet fingertips.

8. Whisk 1 egg yolk with 1 tablespoon of water and brush the pie with this mixture.

9. Put the pie into the oven on a wire rack that is a bit lower than in the middle.

10. Bake for 30–40 minutes. Leave to cool a little and take the pie out of the mold.

Ravlyky — Sweet yeast dough snails

Ingredients

100 ml (½ cup or
3½ fl oz) milk

13 g (½ oz) fresh yeast

80 g (3 oz) butter

3 egg yolks

100 g (3½ oz) sugar

Flour

1 pinch salt

1. Make the dough in the same way as described in the "Granny's pie" recipe above. Roll it out on a floured surface and cut into strips.

2. Sprinkle each strip with sugar and cinnamon on one side.

3. Fold each strip into a spiral resembling a snail ("ravlyk" is Ukrainian for "a snail"). Tuck the ends underneath.

4. Grease the baking tray and place the pastry close to one another. Leave to proof in a warm place for 30–40 minutes. From now on don't touch the dough.

5. Bake at 180 °C (350 °F) for 30 minutes.

Strawberry pies

Ingredients

270 g (9½ oz) flour

7 g (2 tsp) fresh yeast

½ tsp salt

1 tbsp sugar

130 ml (½ cup or 4 fl oz) milk

10 g (⅔ tbsp) butter (room temperature)

400 g (14 oz) strawberriesi

Sugar for the filling

1. Dissolve the yeast in 30 ml (2 tbsp) of warm milk (30–35 °C / 85–95 °F). Combine the flour with salt and 1 tablespoon of sugar. Stir in the yeast and pour in the remaining milk (warm it up a little so that all the ingredients are the same temperature). Mix thoroughly and make a tight dough. Put a piece of warm and soft butter inside and knead for 6–7 minutes until the dough is smooth and stops sticking to your hands or the bowl.

2. Cover with a towel and leave in a warm place to proof. You can also use the oven that you've preheated to 35–40 °C / 95–105 °F (not more) or put the dough next to a radiator or electric heater.

3. Punch down the dough twice — in 40 and 70 minutes. Then let the dough expand 3 times its initial size, which will take another 40– 60 minutes.

4. Divide the dough into 6 equal balls. Take one piece and make it smooth by pulling all the uneven parts and creases downward. Let them proof in a warm place for 15 minutes.

5. Put each ball with the smooth side down and roll them out into circles.

6. Put 1 teaspoon of sugar and 3–4 strawberries in the middle of each circle. Wet the edges with water and pinch to seal. Grease the baking tray with fat or line it with baking paper. Lay the pies on the baking tray and leave for 10–15 minutes. Brush with an egg whisked with 1 tablespoon of water.

7. Preheat the oven to 220 °C (425 °F). Bake the pies for 10–12 minutes.

8. Leave to cool on the baking tray.

Black currant cake

You'll certainly like this delicious cake. Instead of black currant, you can take raisins, nuts, candied fruit or some other berries, but make sure they are not very juicy.

Ingredients

1 egg

100 g (3½ oz) sour cream 20% fat

140 g (5 oz) flour

1 tbsp oil

50 g (3½ tbsp) butter

70 g (5⅔ tbsp) sugar

½ tsp baking soda

Vinegar

1 pinch salt

150 g (5⅓ oz) black currants

1. Combine the egg, sour cream, and cooled melted butter.

2. Sift the flour into another bowl. Add salt and sugar.

3. Take half of the flour and stir it into the egg mixture. Mix everything. Combine the baking soda with the vinegar and pour it into the dough. Add the remaining flour. Mix and add the black currants. Mix very carefully in order not to crush the berries.

4. Grease the baking mold and place the dough inside (the dough must occupy ⅔ of the mold). Bake at 180 °C (350 °F) for 30–35 minutes.

Apple pie

Ingredients

For the pie:

1 egg

80 g (3 oz) butter

40 g (3 tbsp) sugar

160 g (5⅔ oz) flour

½ tsp baking soda

Vinegar

For the filling:

3 big green apples

½ lemon

½ tsp cinnamon

2 tbsp sugar

1 tbsp honey

1. Thoroughly stir the sugar and the soft butter with a spoon or use a food processor. Add the egg, sprinkle with salt, and stir until smooth. Add the flour and the baking soda mixed with the vinegar. Make the dough — elastic, but not too tight.

2. Chill in the fridge for 30 minutes.

3. Mix 2 tablespoons of sugar with 2 tablespoons of water and boil over medium heat until it darkens.

4. Peel 2 apples and dice them into either medium-sized cubes or thick wedges.

5. Combine the syrup, apples, and cinnamon. Boil for 4–5 minutes. The caramel must solidify while the apples must remain crispy. If it hasn't happened, drain the apples, but keep the syrup.

6. Peel the remaining apple, cut in half, and remove the core. Slice the apple very thinly. For that you'd better take a kitchen mandoline or a potato peeler.

7. Drizzle the apple slices with lemon juice and mix carefully.

8. Take the dough out of the fridge, knead a little, and roll it out on a floured table. Fold the dough around the rolling pin and transfer to the baking mold. Trim the edges.

9. Preheat the oven to 180 °C (350 °F).

10. You can shape the pie crust by joining several pieces of dough together and sealing them with your wet hands. The edges can be formed out of small pieces of dough that you can press together with a fork or a wet teaspoon. This will make your pie look very interesting.

11. Prick the pie crust with a fork in several places. Put the apples boiled in the syrup. Place the slices of fresh apple on top. Brush with the remaining caramel.

12. Put the pie into the oven on a wire rack which is a bit lower than the one in the middle. 30 minutes later, brush the cake with honey and bake for another 20 minutes until golden.

13. It takes about 50–60 minutes to bake the pie if the dough is thin and the baking mold is about 21–23 cm (8–9 in) in diameter.

Desserts

Baked apples with walnuts and honey

Ingredients

- **2 big firm apples**
- **2 tbsp honey**
- **70 g (2½ oz) raisins**
- **60 g (2 oz) walnuts**
- **½ tsp ground cinnamon**

1. Cut off the apple tops. Carefully remove the core, using a thin knife and a teaspoon. Be sure you don't pierce the apple, or all the juice will leek while baking.

2. Crush the walnuts with a knife. Set half of the nuts aside. Combine the other half with the raisins, honey and cinnamon.

3. Stuff the apples with this mixture. Put the remaining nuts on top.

4. Preheat the oven to 190 °C (375 °F). Lay the apples on the baking tray. Don't cover them with anything. Bake the apples for about 15 minutes until half-done. The nuts will get slightly brown. Cover the apples with the tops you've cut off. Bake until done.

Baked semolina porridge with cottage cheese and sugar crust

It is a delicious porridge that resembles a dessert. It makes an ideal breakfast and takes very little time to cook. Delicate inside, the porridge has a crunchy top. If you like, you can also add some fruit, raisins or jam.

Ingredients

50 g (1⅔ oz) semolina

300 ml (1⅓ cups or 10 fl oz) milk (2.5–3.2% fat)

60 g (2 oz) cottage cheese (not very wet, approximately 9% fat, not too sour)

1 egg

10 g (¾ tbsp) butter

1 tsp honey

2 tsp sugar

25 g (1 oz) dried apricots

⅓ tsp vanilla sugar

Butter for greasing

1. Make a thick semolina porridge. For that, bring the milk to the boil and add the semolina. Stir constantly to prevent lumps. Reduce the heat. If the porridge thickens too soon while the semolina is not cooked through yet, add some more milk. Cook over very low heat for about 6–7 minutes. The porridge must be very thick in the end. If you have added too much liquid, and the porridge turns out to be too watery, turn up the heat and keep on cooking until it thickens. Be careful and don't let it burn. Add the butter, vanilla sugar, and honey. Stir vigorously with a wooden spoon until the butter melts. Leave for 5 minutes to cool.

2. Cover the dried apricots with boiling water and leave for 10–15 minutes. Drain.

3. When the porridge is ready, add one egg and stir thoroughly with a spoon until the mixture is smooth and uniform. Make sure the porridge is not too hot. Otherwise the egg may get cooked.

4. Prepare baking molds. You can use uncovered pots, low mugs, or ramekins. Grease with butter. First put the cottage cheese. Level and press the cheese with a spoon. Then put a layer or dried apricots (cut into pieces) and pour the semolina porridge on top. Level with a spoon and sprinkle with 2 tablespoons of sugar.

5. Preheat the oven to 210 °C (410 °F). Put the mold on the top rack and bake for 15 minutes until it has formed a golden crust.

Pumpkin pancakes

This is an unusual combination of sweet pumpkin and cinnamon. You can experiment and make pancakes with different flavors. For example, you can add dried berries, serve pancakes with sour cream, make usual pancakes with vanilla flavor, or make plain pancakes and serve them with your favorite jam, rosehip syrup, etc.

Ingredients

90 g (3 oz) pumpkin

180 g (6⅓ oz) milk

30 g (1 oz) butter

190 g (6⅔ oz) flour

1 tbsp sugar

1 egg

½ tsp baking soda

Vinegar or lemon juice

1 tsp sugar

½ tsp cinnamon

¼ tsp salt

1. Peel the pumpkin, cut into pieces to make it cook faster, put into a baking mold, cover with a lid and bake at 180 °C (350 °F) for 1 hour until tender. Then mash it with a fork and leave to cool.

2. Sift the flour, mix with sugar, salt, and cinnamon.

3. In a separate bowl, combine the egg, milk, and puréed pumpkin. Transfer to the bowl with the flour.

4. Stir until uniform. Add the butter (melted but not hot) and the baking soda mixed with vinegar or lemon juice.

5. Heat the frying pan. Drizzle with a little oil every time you fry a new pancake. It is very important to use as little oil as possible — the frying pan must remain almost dry. A cast iron frying pan will be the best choice for making these pancakes.

6. Generously spoon the batter on the frying pan. Slightly flatten the pancakes with a spoon so that the middle is thin and cooks through well. Fry the pancakes over medium heat. Turn when you see bubbles all over the surface.

7. Stack the pancakes on individual plates. Put a lump of tasty butter and pour honey or syrup on top because the pancakes are not very sweet on their own. Rather than eating one pancake at a time, it's much tastier to eat them all at once, cutting the stack as if it were a cake!

Apple and walnut pancakes

Ingredients

For the pancakes:

2 eggs

100 g (3½ oz) flour

170 ml (¾ cup or 5¾ fl oz) milk 2.5% fat

50 ml (3⅓ tbsp or 2 fl oz) kefir (or liquid drinkable yogurt)

1 tbsp sugar

Pinch of salt

1 tbsp oil

1 tbsp butter

For the filling:

2 apples

75 g (2⅔ oz) raisins

75 g (2⅔ oz) walnuts

6 tbsp sugar

100 ml (½ cup or 3½ fl oz) water

1 tsp cinnamon

1. Combine the eggs, sugar, salt, and flour. Add the milk in small portions, each time stirring thoroughly. Add the kefir and the oil. Stir to get rid of any lumps.

2. Fry pancakes on a cast iron frying pan about 18 cm (7 in) in diameter. Grease the pan with oil every other time, using a brush or a halved potato pierced on a fork.

3. Stack the pancakes and grease the edges with butter.

4. Peel the apples and dice into large cubes. Crush the nuts with a knife.

5. Mix the sugar with the water and boil over medium heat until it darkens. Add the apples, walnuts, raisins and cinnamon. At first, the caramel will thicken a bit, but then it will become liquid again. Turn up the heat to the maximum and boil for 4–5 minutes.

6. Plate up the pancakes. Put a spoonful of the filling in the middle of each pancake and fold three times. You can also serve them with a scoop of ice-cream.

Yummy poppy seed pancakes

Ingredients

For the pancakes:

60 g (2 oz) flour

1 egg

100 ml (½ cup or 3½ fl oz) kefir (or liquid drinkable yogurt)

50 ml (3⅓ tbsp or 2 fl oz) milk

½ tsp baking soda

1 tbsp oil

Pinch of salt

1 tsp sugar

For the filling:

50 g (1⅔ oz) poppy seeds

400 ml (1¾ cups or 14 fl oz) water

40 g (1½ oz) sugar

30 g (2 tbsp) butter

1. Cover the poppy seeds with 200 ml (1 cup or 7 fl oz) of boiling water and leave for 1 hour.

2. Combine the eggs, sugar, salt, flour, and baking soda. Add the milk and stir to get rid of any lumps. Add the kefir and the oil. Mix thoroughly.

3. Fry pancakes on a cast iron frying pan about 18 cm (7 in) in diameter. Grease the pan with oil every other time, using a brush or a halved potato pierced on a fork.

4. Stack the pancakes and grease the edges with butter.

5. Drain the poppy seeds and crush them in a mortar. You can also put them through a meat grinder or use a blender. Cover with 200 ml (1 cup or 7 fl oz) of boiling water one more time, add the sugar and boil for 30–40 minutes until the mixture gets really thick. The end result should look like caramel with poppy seeds. Stir in the butter. Use immediately before the filling solidifies.

6. Put a spoonful of the filling on a pancake, spread evenly, tuck the edges and roll. Cut in two pieces diagonally.

Cherry varenyky

You can make cherry varenyky with frozen pitted cherries. If you use fresh cherries, you'd better leave the stones. Otherwise you will have too much cherry juice.

Ingredients

For dough:

120 ml (½ cup, 4 fl oz) water

200 g (7 oz) all-purpose flour

20 g (1 tbsp) butter

2 pinches of salt

For filling:

700 g (1 lb 9 oz) cherries

Sugar

Sour cream, honey, and butter for serving

1. Mix the flour and salt in a large bowl. Bring the water to a boil along with the butter. Then pour this into the flour in a thin stream and stir with a spoon. Hand knead for 3-5 minutes. Start gently, as the dough will be hot at first. Wrap the dough in plastic wrap and leave on the table for 30 minutes.

2. Remove the pits from the cherries. But you can leave the pits in the cherries.

3. Divide the dough into 2–3 pieces to make it easier to roll out. Roll out the dough very thinly and cut out circles 7–10 cm (2⅔ – 4 in) in diameter. You can use a special cutter or a regular glass to do so. You will need to cut out smaller circles if you like small varenyky with only 2 cherries inside. Or you can make some really big varenyky with 5–6 cherries.

4. Take a dough circle in one hand. First, sprinkle in a bit of sugar with a teaspoon (½ – ⅔ tsp). The sugar must be sprinkled on first so that it does not get into the seam later.

5. Place as many cherries as you can, usually 5–7, and pinch the edges together well, starting from the closest edge. If the dough has been on the table for a long time and is slightly dry, moisten the edges with cold water before adding sugar.

6. Bring plenty of water to a boil. Cook the varenyky in batches. Check all edges again before tossing them into the water. Add the varenyky, cover to bring the water to a boil quickly, and cook for no more than 2 minutes. The dough is very thin and the varenyky will cook quickly.

7. Serve with sour cream, butter, and honey or sugar. Eat right away!

Lazy varenyky

Ingredients

350 g (12½ oz) dry and soft farmer's (curd) cheese, 5-10% fat

2 tbsp sugar

2 tbsp all-purpose flour

1 egg yolk

Salt

1 tbsp butter

Jam or honey

Sour cream or Greek yogurt

1. Put the farmer's cheese into a food processor, add the egg yolk, sugar, flour, and a pinch of salt. Blend for a short time, 20–30 seconds, so that the dough doesn't turn "rubbery." You can use a mixer.

2. Shape the dough into rolls about 4 cm (1½ in) in diameter. Cut into pieces 1½ cm (½ in) long. Or form the dough into balls using a teaspoon. Roll between your palms.

3. Bring 2 liters of water to a boil. Add a pinch of salt. Drop the dumplings into the boiling water. Stir gently to avoid them sticking to the bottom. Cover with a lid to bring the water back to a boil more quickly and cook them until they float.

4. Using a slotted spoon, transfer the dumplings to a plate, add a pat of butter. Serve with sour cream, your favorite jam, or honey.

Pumpkin puree with raisins and rice

Ingredients

300 g (10½ oz) pumpkin

40 g (1½ oz) rice

30 g (1 oz) raisins

200 ml (1 cup or 7 fl oz) water

200 ml (1 cup or 7 fl oz) milk 2.5% fat

1 tbsp sugar

15 g (1 tbsp) butter

Salt

1. Peel the pumpkin and grate using large holes. Cover with the water, bring to a boil and cook over low heat for 15 minutes.

2. Wash the rice several times until the water is transparent.

3. Add the milk, salt, sugar, and rice. Cook for 25 minutes until the rice is done. All the liquid must evaporate by the end. If there is too little liquid but the rice hasn't cooked yet, add more milk.

4. At the very end stir in the raisins and a lump of butter.

5. Leave covered for 15 minutes.

Semolina porridge with cherry kyssil

Ingredients

60 g (2 oz) semolina

540 ml (2 ⅓ cups or 18⅓ fl oz) milk 2.5% fat

1½ tbsp sugar

30 g butter

100 g (3½ oz) pitted cherries (frozen cherries are fine)

200 ml (1 cup or 7 fl oz) water

2 tsp starch

1. Make a thick semolina porridge. For that, bring the milk to the boil, add the semolina, and cook for 2–3 minutes until done, stirring constantly.

2. Add ½ tablespoon of sugar and butter. Stir vigorously with a wooden spoon until smooth. Plate up immediately.

3. Make kyssil. For that, combine the sugar with the cherries and water. Bring to a boil and add the starch mixed with 2 tablespoons of water.

4. Reduce the heat and bring to a boil, stirring constantly. When kyssil becomes less turbid and thickens (1–2 minutes after starting to boil), remove from the heat. Pour over the porridge and serve.

Barley porridge with berries

Ingredients

- 200 g (7 oz) pearl barley
- 500 ml (2 cups or 1 pt) milk
- 80 g (3 oz) butter
- 1 tbsp sugar
- Water
- 400 g (14 oz) berries (strawberries, black currants, blueberries, blackberries, cherries)

1. Thoroughly wash the barley and soak overnight.

2. Drain the next day and pour in 100 ml (½ cup or 3½ fl oz) of milk and water to cover the surface. Cook over very low heat, adding milk when necessary.

3. Cook until done. Add sugar and butter in the end and stir vigorously with a spoon. The porridge must get a bit whiter.

4. Leave covered for 15 minutes.

5. Plate up, adding a lump of butter and berries.

Carrot and cheese pudding

Ingredients

400 g (14 oz) cottage cheese

1 medium-sized carrot

60 g (2 oz) semolina

30 ml (2 tbsp) milk

3 tbsp sugar

1 egg

⅓ tsp salt

10 g (½ tbsp) butter

1. Boil the carrot until tender and grate finely. Combine with the cheese and stir thoroughly.

2. Soak the semolina in milk for 30 minutes. Whisk the eggs with sugar and salt. Mix everything.

3. Grease a baking mold or a baking sheet with butter. Put the pudding and smooth out the surface. Don't make the pudding too thick.

4. Preheat the oven to 200 °C (390 °F) and bake the pudding for 25–35 minutes until the crust is golden. Don't open the oven. Leave to cool.

5. Serve with sour cream or caramelized apples.

Cheese hombovtsi with fruit sauce

Ingredients

260 g (9 oz) fat dry farmer's cottage cheese

70 g (2½ oz) semolina

1 egg

6 tbsp sugar

200 g (7 oz) of various berries (frozen berries are also fine, such as strawberry, raspberry, pitted cherry, bilberry, wild strawberry, black and red currant, blueberry or blackberry)

1 level tbsp potato starch

1. If the cheese is not soft enough, thoroughly stir it with a spoon or pass it through a sieve. Add the semolina, 2 tablespoons of sugar, and the egg. Mix everything thoroughly, cover with a lid, and leave in the fridge for 30–40 minutes to let the mixture swell. It is important.

2. Cover the berries with 4 tablespoons of sugar and leave for 20 minutes. Add ½ glass of water and bring to a boil over high heat. Dissolve the starch in 2 tablespoons of water and add it to the berries. Reduce the heat and stir constantly. Once the berries start boiling again, the juice, which has become cloudy because of the starch, must become transparent again and start getting thicker. Keep on stirring. Cook for another ½ minutes and remove from the heat. The sauce must not be too thick. Cover with a lid so that a starch film does not form on the surface.

3. Take the dough out of the fridge and make balls about 4 cm (1½ in) in diameter (with this amount of dough you'll get 4 balls). Smooth out the surface with your wet hands.

4. Plunge into boiling water, let them appear on the surface and cook for another 2 minutes. Plate up and pour with berry sauce.

Pancakes with cheese

Ingredients

2 eggs

120 g (4 oz) flour

200 ml (1 cup or 7 fl oz) milk 2.5% fat

80 ml (⅓ cup or 2¾ fl oz) water

2½ tbsp butter

2 tbsp sugar

¼ tsp salt

400 g (14 oz) soft and fat farmer's cottage cheese with raisins

1. Combine the eggs with salt and 1 tablespoon of sugar. Add the flour, mix, and pour in half of the milk. Mix again and pour in the remaining milk and water. Add 1½ tablespoons of melted (not hot) butter. Stir the batter with a ladle, scooping and pouring the batter back into the bowl from higher up. This will aerate the batter and make it more watery, which will help to make really thin pancakes.

2. Fry pancakes on a cast iron frying pan about 18 cm (7 in) in diameter. Grease the pan with oil every other time, using a brush or a halved potato pierced on a fork.

3. Stack the pancakes on a plate and cover with a lid.

4. Place the pancake with the brown side up. Put 1 tablespoon of the filling (about 25 g / 1 oz) on each pancake and fold.

5. Put the stuffed pancakes into a baking mold, brush with the remaining melted butter and sprinkle with sugar.

6. Bake at 220 °C (425 °F) for 15 minutes until golden.

Syrnyk

It is a delicious and delicate cheese cake with a pleasant buttery flavor. Be sure to take low fat cheese (9 %) and tasty 82% fat butter with a rich, creamy taste. You can also add raisins, diced dried apricots or some lemon zest.

Ingredients

For filling:

500 g (1 lb) farmer's cottage (curd) cheese

4 eggs

1 glass sugar

2 tsp vanilla sugar

For the dough:

260 g (9 oz) flour

4 tbsp sugar

120 g (4 oz) very cold butter

1 tsp baking soda

¼ tsp salt

1. Pass the cheese through a sieve or use a blender. Combine with the eggs, sugar, and vanilla sugar and stir thoroughly until smooth. You can also use a blender for that.

2. Make the dough. In a separate dish combine the sugar, flour, and baking soda. Grate the cold butter into the mixture. Manually rub the butter with the flour and sugar until the mixture resembles breadcrumbs.

3. Grease the baking mold (about 20 x 25 cm / 8 x 10 in) with butter.

4. Put ⅔ of the dough into the mold and spread evenly. Don't press.

5. Put the cheese mixture on the dough and put the remaining dough on top.

6. Bake at 180 °C (350 °F) for 40–60 minutes until golden. Don't open the oven during the first 40 minutes.

7. Leave to cool to let the core thicken. Wait for 2–3 hours and serve. Syrnyk tastes even better on the next day.

Lviv syrnyk

Ingredients

For the syrnyk:

500 g (1 lb) fat farmer's cottage (curd) cheese (not too wet)

4 eggs

100 g (3½ oz) butter

100 g (3½ oz) sugar

100 g (3½ oz) raisins

1 lemon

1 tbsp flour

Vanilla

For the glaze:

2 tbsp fat sour cream

2 tbsp cocoa

2 tbsp sugar

1. Pass the cottage cheese through a sieve or use a blender. Combine the cheese with the sugar, egg yolks, lemon zest, and soft butter. Add the juice of ⅙ of the lemon. Mix everything.

2. Preheat the oven to 180 °C (350 °F).

3. Whip the egg whites until stiff peaks form. Add them to the cheese mixture and carefully stir with a wooden spoon.

4. Grease the baking mold with butter and dust with flour. Put the dough into the mold and place it on a wire rack which is a bit lower than in the middle.

5. Bake for 50 minutes without opening the oven. Turn off the heat and leave the cake in the oven for another 3–4 hours.

6. Make the glaze. In a saucepan, combine the sugar, cocoa and sour cream. Bring to a boil, reduce the heat, and simmer for 3–4 minutes, stirring constantly until thickened.

7. Turn the cake upside down on a plate. Pour the glaze over the cake and chill in the fridge overnight.

8. Serve syrnyk on the next day.

Fluffy cheese pudding

It is a very delicate, light and fluffy pudding. Eggs are very important for the recipe as they cause the pudding to rise. So it's better not to reduce the number of eggs. The pudding is very easy to make. Make sure you only use fat free (0 %) cheese for this recipe and thoroughly stir all the components until smooth.

Ingredients

500 g (1 lb) fat farmer's cottage (curd) cheese (not too wet)

100 g (3½ oz) butter

100 g (3½ oz) sugar

4 eggs

½ lemon

50 g (1⅔ oz) semolina

1 tbsp powdered sugar

1. Preheat the oven to 180 °C (350 °F). Zest the lemon and squeeze the juice.

2. Mash the cheese, blend in a blender or pass through a sieve. It is important to make it as smooth as possible.

3. Bring the butter to room temperature and stir it with the sugar, lemon zest, and juice. Add the eggs (one at a time) and stir until smooth.

4. Mix with the cheese and the semolina.

5. Grease the baking mold with butter. Put the cheese mixture inside and smooth out the surface.

6. Bake for 50–60 minutes. Don't open the oven during the first 40 minutes. Leave to cool, take the pudding out of the mold and sprinkle it with powdered sugar.

Syrnyky

Ingredients

350 g (12½ oz) dry and soft farmer's (curd) cheese (5-10% fat)

1 egg yolk

1 tbsp sugar

1 heaping tbsp all-purpose flour

1 tsp vanilla sugar

Pinch of salt

Zest of ½ lemon

Sour cream for serving

½ cup dusting flour

Sunflower oil or other vegetable oil for frying

1. Zest half a lemon using a fine grater and a special knife. Mince finely.

2. In a food processor, combine the farmer's cheese, egg yolk, sugar, vanilla sugar, salt, zest, and flour. Use a dough mixer, if available. Blend for about 20 seconds.

3. Form the dough into balls, with each weighing 50 g (2 oz). This comes out to about a full tablespoon of dough. Sprinkle flour on your work surface. Roll each syrnyk lightly in flour, and press down on the top of each with a knife.

4. Use a knife to evenly form the sides of the syrnyky. Take a knife in one hand and place it on the sides of the syrnyk. With your other hand, hold the cheese patty with the lower part of your palm and roll.

5. Preheat a non-stick skillet. Heat 2–3 tablespoons of vegetable oil and add the syrnyky. Cook over low heat until golden brown. Turn over and cook the other side until golden brown. Remove from the skillet and place on a paper towel to absorb excess oil.

6. Serve with sour cream and honey.

Cherry kyssil

Ingredients

250 g (9 oz) cherries

1 L (4 cups or 2 pt) water

40 g (1½ oz or 3 tbsp) sugar

2 level tbsp potato starch

1. In a saucepan, combine the cherries and the sugar. Pour in ½ glass of water and bring to a boil. Crush the cherries with a spoon and pour in the remaining water. Cook for 10 minutes.

2. Dissolve the starch in ½ glass of cold water and pour into the boiling mixture. Stir constantly to prevent any lumps. Simmer for 2 minutes.

Beverages

Mint and strawberry drink

Ingredients

300 g (10½ oz) strawberries

1 bunch mint

3 tbsp sugar

1 L (4 cups or 2 pt) water

½ lemon

1. Put the strawberries into a pot, combine with sugar, and leave for 20 minutes. Crush the berries with a fork. Add the mint (only the leaves).

2. Cover with boiling water and bring to a boil. Leave to cool with the lid on. Add lemon juice and strain.

Morse — cranberry drink

Ingredients

500 g cranberries

1½ L (6 cups or 3 pt) water

100 g (3½ oz) sugar

1. Sort out the cranberries, wash thoroughly, and crush with sugar.

2. Cover with water, bring almost to a boil, but do not boil.

3. Remove from the heat and leave to cool.

4. Strain the drink. Keep in a non-transparent bottle.

Uzvar – dried fruits compote

Ingredients

350 g (12 oz) dried fruit

30 g (1 oz) raisins

2½ L (10½ cups or 5⅓ pt) boiled water

100 g (3½ oz) sugar

1. Sort out the dried fruit and wash thoroughly.

2. Combine the dried fruit, raisins and sugar. Cover with water.

3. Bring to a boil, remove from the heat, and leave covered until it cools down.

4. Strain.

Rosehip drink

Ingredients

100 g (3 ½ oz) dried rosehips

1 L (4 cups or 2 pt) water

70 g (2½ oz) sugar

1. Thoroughly wash the rosehips and cover with 200 ml (1 cup or 7 fl oz) of boiling water. Leave for 2 hours.

2. Put the rosehips through a meat grinder or use a blender.

3. Cover the crushed rosehips with 800 ml (3 cups or 27 fl oz) of boiling water. Add the sugar.

4. If you can, brew the drink in a thermos or in a different closed vessel until it cools down.

5. Strain through several layers of cheesecloth.

Don't leave the crushed rosehips in the drink. The berries contain numerous small hairs that irritate the throat and the skin.

Carpaty

Ingredients

150 g (5⅓ oz) black currants

2 tbsp sugar

½ lemon

1 L (4 cups or 2 pt) water

1. Bring the water to a boil, add sugar, and leave to cool.

2. Crush the black currants or blend in a blender. Cover with the cool sugary water, add lemon juice, mix thoroughly, and leave for 15 minutes.

3. Filter and serve cold.

You can also add honey if you like.

This will make this drink even healthier.

Strawberry spotykach

Ingredients

500 g (1 lb) strawberries

300 g (10½ oz) sugar

500 ml (2 cups or 1 pt) horilka (vodka)

1. Thoroughly wash the strawberries, cover with 100 g (3½ oz) sugar, and leave for 1 hour to let the juice appear.

2. Make syrup with 200 g (7 oz) sugar and 200 ml (1 cup or 7 fl oz) water. When it starts to darken, pour in the strawberry juice and remove from the heat. Transfer into a clean glass jar, pour in horilka (vodka), cover with a lid, and let it infuse for 2—3 days.

3. Strain and transfer the drink into a pot. Bring it almost to a boil over very low heat. Don't let it boil though. Stir, simmer for 3 minutes, and remove from the heat. Pour into bottles and chill.

Tsytrynivka

1 L (4 cups or 2 pt) horilka (vodka)

3 lemons

2 tbsp sugar

1. Thoroughly wash and zest the lemons.
   Put the lemon zest into a clean glass jar or a bottle.

2. Make syrup with 2 tablespoons of sugar and
   2 tablespoons of water. Cover the lemon zest with
   100 ml (½ cup or 3½ fl oz) of boiling water, add
   the syrup and leave to cool.

3. Plunge 1 lemon in boiling water, slice, and put into
   the vessel. Squeeze the juice out of the remaining
   2 lemons.

4. Pour horilka (vodka) into the vessel and add the lemon
   juice.

5. Infuse for 3 days at least (better for a week).

Made in the USA
Las Vegas, NV
16 February 2024

85855178R10122